The AMERICAN REVOLUTION

"Stand your ground! Don't fire unless fired upon.
But if they want to have a war, let it begin here!"

—Captain Jonas Parker at the Battle of Lexington,
April 19, 1775

More Landmarks in History

The AMERICAN REVOLUTION

by Bruce Bliven, Jr.

Random House 🏠 New York

For Mary Hackett Swope

Library of Congress Cataloging-in-Publication Data
Bliven, Bruce. The American Revolution.
Reprint of the 1958 ed. published by Random House, New
York, in series: Landmark books. Includes index.
SUMMARY: Presents an account of events leading up to and
occurring during the American Revolution.
1. United States–History–Revolution, 1775–1783–Juvenile litera-
ture. [1. United States–History–Revolution, 1775–1783]
I. Title. [E208.B66 1981] 973.3 80-20813
ISBN: 0-394-84696-6 (pbk.) ISBN: 0-394-90383-8 (lib. bdg.)

Printed in the United States of America
25 24 23 22 21 20

LANDMARK BOOKS is a trademark of Random House, Inc.

❧ Contents

❧ The ❧
American Revolution

৯ 1
A Young King Ends a Great War

When the American Revolution began, Americans were subjects of the King of England, who lived three thousand miles (and at least six weeks' sailing time) away from them.

When the Revolution ended, Americans were citizens of a new nation, the United States of America. American laws were made on American soil, and they were administered by men American citizens had elected.

The change was truly revolutionary, yet it is hard to set an exact date for the beginning of the American Revolution. It certainly began long before the Revolutionary War, which lasted from 1775 to 1783.

A wise observer, John Adams of Massachusetts, one of the Revolution's leaders and later the second President of the United States, wrote: "The Revolution was in the minds and hearts of the people, and this was effected from 1760 to 1775, in the course of fifteen years, before a drop of blood was shed. . . ."

What happened in those fifteen years?

In October 1760 a very important event took place. A plump, popeyed twenty-two-year-old became King of England. He was stubborn George III, who was sure that kings never made mistakes. He was destined to become the last monarch to rule over America.

When George became King, England was fighting—and winning—a global war against France. The two countries, with their allies, were battling on the continent of Europe, in India, in the West Indies and all over the Seven Seas. They were fighting in North America, too. The French held Canada and a large territory west of the Mississippi River called Louisiana—far larger than the State of Louisiana today. The British held thirteen colonies: Massachusetts, New Hampshire, Connecticut, Rhode Island, New York, Pennsylvania, New Jersey, Delaware, Maryland, Virginia, North Carolina, South Carolina, and Georgia. For seven years, starting in 1755, British soldiers and Americans, fighting together, fought against the French and their Indian allies.

England was beating France, and that pleased young George III. But he had political plans of his own which made him want to end the war fast.

All during his boyhood, George's mother had said to him, over and over, "George, be a King!" It was exactly what he meant to be, now that he wore the crown. However, his power as King was not clearly defined. For more than a century the English people had been fighting their way toward self-government, toward making their own laws in Parliament, the English counterpart of our Congress.

George realized that he was limited in whatever he might want to do by what Parliament wanted. He knew that he couldn't ignore Parliament. King Charles I had been beheaded in 1649, and King James II, his son, had been overthrown in 1688 for trying to rule without Parliament.

George III did not want to repeat their mistake. But he did think he could "be a King" *through* Parliament—by influencing and controlling the lawmaking body, buying votes with bribes and giving government jobs to men who voted his way.

In order to try that plan, George had to get rid of the brilliant war leader Prime Minister William Pitt, whose popularity and independence stood in the way of any scheme to increase the King's power.

Therefore the King's faction in Parliament voted to end the war that had made Pitt famous and powerful. The peace treaty was signed in 1763. The French lost Canada, which was given to England. Spain got France's Louisiana territory. The American colonists were delighted to be rid of powerful France, for she had not only stood in the way of American dreams about settling the West, but also had hired Indians to wipe out American frontier villages.

Once George had beaten Pitt on the question of continuing the war, and gotten rid of him, he was forever changing prime ministers. In the next nine years he tried new ones constantly. It was hard to find a man willing to obey George's wishes who could also get along with Parliament and remain popular with English voters.

And Parliament, led by a procession of weak prime ministers, made some strange moves.

The Americans, puzzled at first, soon grew angry at the odd actions of Parliament and George's various ministers—not guessing, for a long time, that some of the most annoying actions were really their King's ideas.

Even under ideal circumstances, of course, it would have been almost impossible for a few hundred men, most of whom had never seen America, to meet in London and make good laws for the thirteen colonies. And the circumstances —a stubborn King and a partly corrupt Parliament—were far from ideal.

Americans were loyal to their King. And, thinking that Parliament, not the King, was responsible for the mistakes in colonial policy, they did not feel they were disloyal when they disobeyed English laws that rubbed them the wrong way.

❧ 2
Quarrels over Money

The Americans began by disobeying laws that had to do with money.

The Seven Years' War had cost fortunes. Its expense had been one of George III's main arguments for ending it. English taxes were sky-high and England's war debt was huge.

Lord Grenville, who became Prime Minister in 1763, was a penny pincher. It didn't take much imagination for him to think of raising money in America. There was talk of keeping a British army of 10,000 on the American frontier to protect the colonies from Indians, talk that had been stirred up by an Indian uprising led by a chief named Pontiac, shortly after the 1763 peace treaty.

Grenville thought the Americans should start to pay for this British army that might be sent to America, and he began by trying to enforce some old laws called the Acts of Trade and Navigation. These had never been seriously enforced before.

The Acts included taxes, payable to Great

Britain, on imports shipped into colonial harbors. They also restricted the places in the world where American ships, laden with American produce, could go to sell their cargoes.

Even a small tax on a single item like molasses —which mostly came from the French West Indies—could practically ruin business in Boston. Massachusetts and, indeed, most of New England is not very good farmland, and the colonies were forbidden by law to manufacture and sell such things as china, metal implements and cloth that might compete with goods made in England. Therefore, one of the few profitable things the people around Boston could do was distill rum. Rum is made from molasses.

If the British really collected the molasses import tax, and the distillers had to add that amount to the price of rum, New England rum would be enough more expensive so that nobody would buy it. And without rum to ship, Boston —the busy seaport for a great part of New England—might become a ghost town.

That was only one example.

All the colonies were hurt in various ways, depending on what they produced. When anything upset America's import-export business, on which so much depended, it also upset almost every American's ability to earn a living.

The taxes were bad. The restrictions on trade were bad. Even worse, from the Americans' point of view, was the method by which the Acts were supposed to be enforced.

The King's Custom Offices in American ports were enlarged and filled with Englishmen who came across the Atlantic hoping to make lots of money at the job. To the colonists' disgust, both the customs officers who made arrests and the judges of the courts that found American shippers guilty of "smuggling" were entitled to a percentage of the value of the ship and its cargo, which were seized by the government and sold.

"Smuggler" has a wicked sound, but in the 1760s the word was applied to all Americans who defied what they regarded as preposterous Acts. Some of the shippers found guilty were doubtless innocent. You can imagine what a court would be like in which the police and the judge profited to the tune of several thousand dollars when they found a prisoner guilty!

To make matters worse, Lord Grenville had another money-raising idea: to tax a variety of papers—legal documents, newspapers, marriage licenses, college diplomas, ships' papers and a good many others. Starting in 1765, such papers had to carry a large blue paper seal called a stamp—a revenue stamp—as proof that a tax had been paid.

The stamps were expensive. Furthermore, they denied a right that Americans treasured—the right to fix their own "internal" taxes. Matters like marriage licenses and college diplomas had nothing whatever to do with the British Empire's economics. They were purely American affairs, and British interference—in the shape of that hated blue stamp—seemed obnoxious. In addition to a governor who was, in most cases, appointed by the King, each of the thirteen colonies had an Assembly, or legislature, elected by the people. These Assemblies, most Americans believed, had the right to decide on local taxes. In England, after a long fight, Parliament had won control of taxation. Americans, as British subjects living abroad, felt that their own legislatures should control American taxes. Or, as the popular rallying cry said it: "No taxation without representation!"

Neither the King, nor his ministers, nor even Parliament agreed.

They all thought that the colonial Assemblies could not possibly be compared to the British Parliament, and they denied the American argument completely.

It was a serious difference of opinion, and it led to violence.

A group of prominent colonists held an orderly Stamp Act Congress in New York City to protest the new law, but at the same time angry mobs of citizens rioted in the American seaport towns. The Stamp Masters—the men in each port who were supposed to sell the stamps—were threatened.

Some of their houses were burned down. Even the houses of people who were merely thought to approve of the Stamp Act were set on fire. The Maryland Stamp Master was so frightened by the mob that he fled all the way to New York City, only to discover that the New Yorkers were as menacing as the Marylanders had been.

The protesters' speeches were more violent than their actions. They didn't actually kill anybody. Still, no one dared sell or buy stamps. And since no ship could leave an American port for England without properly stamped papers, trade across the Atlantic came to a standstill.

In July of 1765 Lord Rockingham succeeded Grenville as Prime Minister. He could see that the Stamp Act was costing money instead of making it, but he hated to admit that unruly American rioters had managed to wreck the stamp tax.

Rather cleverly, Lord Rockingham talked to the London merchants who traded with America and persuaded them to ask for the Stamp Act's repeal because it was hurting English business. The merchants complained to Parliament. And in 1766 Parliament—pretending solemnly that it was moved only by London's well-behaved, law-abiding businessmen—repealed the Stamp Act.

❧ 3
Americans Boycott British Goods

At the news that Parliament had repealed the Stamp Act, America went wild with joy. The colonists lit bonfires, rang bells, shot off fireworks and held gay parties. Several cities ordered handsome statues of King George III for their public parks.

In their happy excitement Americans completely overlooked a new law, the Declaratory Act, which Parliament passed at the same time it repealed the Stamp Act. In principle the Declaratory Act was worse than the old law, for it said that Parliament had the power to write laws for the colonies *"in all cases whatsoever"*—which naturally included the power to write tax laws, both internal and external.

In short, the Declaratory Act made a law out of something the Stamp Act had only implied—a principle more hateful, in the long run, than even the despised blue stamps.

But for the time being Americans felt that the lifting of an unfair set of taxes was a great relief.

England's budget problems, on the other hand, were as much of a headache as ever. The American colonies were proving a poor source of income for the Exchequer, as the British call their treasury. English land taxes remained frightfully high. And there was considerable grumbling.

King George, as usual, changed prime ministers. The new man was old William Pitt—the same William Pitt who had been squeezed out of office only five years earlier. At that time the King had been jealous of Pitt's enormous popularity and his great influence in Parliament. Now the King hoped to use exactly those qualities on his own behalf.

But Pitt's great days were over. He was sick and spent only a little time at his job. In his absence, younger cabinet ministers took over. Among them was the chancellor of the exchequer, Charles Townshend. When Parliament decided to reduce the English land tax, thereby reducing the government's income, Townshend had to think of some other way of raising money.

Like Grenville before him, Townshend thought of America. On his suggestion, Parliament passed a new set of taxes for Americans to pay. They were import duties, taxes on shipments from England coming into American ports. The list included paper, paint, glass, lead and tea.

The Townshend duties were just as unpopular in America as Grenville's earlier taxes had been.

To make matters worse, that same year, 1767, Parliament ordered the suspension of the New York Assembly. The New York legislature had refused to obey an order to pay the costs of keeping a few British soldiers in New York City. It regarded the order as an invisible Parliamentary tax. New Yorkers didn't mind having the soldiers in town. What they wanted was the right to vote to pay for them. In the end, rather than do without an Assembly, the New Yorkers gave in and obeyed the order.

The next year the British acted with similar contempt toward the Massachusetts Assembly. The Massachusetts legislators had passed resolutions which—despite England's Declaratory Act —insisted that Parliament did not have the right to tax Americans. London ordered the governor of Massachusetts, the King's representative, to tell the Massachusetts Assembly to take back its resolves. The Assembly refused to do anything of the kind, and the governor dissolved it.

The people in New York and Massachusetts resented Parliament's high-handed attitude toward the colonial legislatures. They resented the new Townshend duties. As a protest, the citizens of all the colonies agreed not to buy any English paper, paint, glass, lead or tea—or, in fact, any English manufactured products at all.

The boycott meant sacrifices on the Americans'

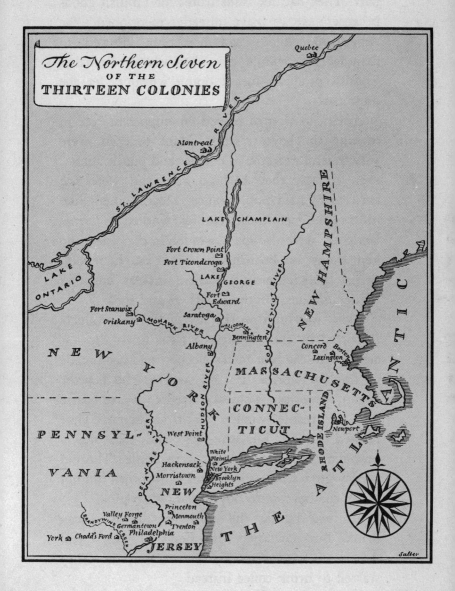

The Northern Seven
OF THE
THIRTEEN COLONIES

Quebec

Montreal

ST. LAWRENCE RIVER

LAKE CHAMPLAIN

Fort Crown Point
Fort Ticonderoga
LAKE GEORGE
Fort Edward
Saratoga
WALLOOMSAC
Bennington

NEW HAMPSHIRE

LAKE ONTARIO

Fort Stanwix
Oriskany
MOHAWK RIVER

Albany

Concord
Lexington
Boston

MASSACHUSETTS

NEW

YORK

HUDSON RIVER

CONNECTICUT RIVER

CONNEC-
TICUT

PENNSYL-

VANIA

DELAWARE RIVER

West Point

White Plains
Hackensack   New York
Morristown   Brooklyn
              Heights

RHODE ISLAND
Newport

THE ATLANTIC

NEW

Princeton   Menmouth
Valley Forge Germantown Trenton
BRANDYWINE CREEK
York Chadd's Ford Philadelphia

JERSEY

Salter

part. They had few substitutes for English goods because, as we have already mentioned, the American colonies had not been allowed to manufacture things for themselves. Refusing English products meant doing without, for the most part.

American women played an important role in making the boycott work. Many of them were very much interested in politics and public affairs, even though they had no vote and were not entitled to hold public office. Most women, like most of the men in the colonies, worked on farms. But there were also many women in the cities who kept shops, ran boarding houses or taught school. British policies outraged them just as much as their husbands, brothers, fathers and sons.

Cloth was high on the list of British products imported by the colonies. All the finest dresses, along with the best men's clothes, had been made of English fabrics. But as soon as the boycott began, American women started to weave coarse but serviceable woolen cloth at home. They refused to use English pins, and that was a problem. Homemade pins were crude. The old supply grew scarce. But American women did not break the boycott to buy new English pins.

Tea was by far the most popular American drink. But now that Townshend had taxed tea, American housewives refused to buy it. They started to drink coffee instead.

The nonimportation agreements, as the boycott was called, caused Americans real hardships.

By now, nine years after George III's accession to the throne, many Americans were almost desperate. Feeling that British policies were ruining America, they were ready to try almost anything.

In Virginia, for instance, George Washington was deeply disturbed by Great Britain's acts. His difficulties were typical of those of all the big planters in the rich, flat lowlands that lie between Virginia's wide rivers—the James, the York, the Rappahannock and the Potomac. Washington's cash crop, like his neighbors', was tobacco. A Virginia plantation owner had to sell his tobacco to an English merchant. It was against the law to sell to a merchant of any other nationality.

The planter had nothing to say about price. That was decided in England. He simply shipped over his crop, usually with a letter to the merchant he dealt with, listing the things he hoped to buy with the money the tobacco brought. These might be luxuries such as elaborate carriages, fine silks and beautiful china, or necessities such as hoes, guns and writing paper. (Speaking, that is, of the days before the boycott.)

The merchants in England sometimes replied that the Virginia tobacco had not sold for a high enough price to pay for the things the planters had ordered. And if the English agent filled the order anyhow, as he usually did, the Virginia planter found himself in debt.

Being in debt was a nightmare. Wealthy colonists—wealthy, that is, according to the total value of the property they owned—were unable to pay their debts because money was so scarce.

The currency shortage, too, was a result of Parliamentary policy. Parliament had forbidden the Assemblies of the various colonies to issue paper money, which might have eased the scarcity. Yet, in the trade with England, America was constantly coming out on the short end, and needed gold or silver to make up the difference. English taxes, like the Townshend duties, had to be paid in gold and silver. British policies drained the gold and silver out of America and left the colonists with no way of getting any.

The situation was absurd and infuriating. By the 1760s currency was so scarce in Virginia that Washington and his neighbors were reduced to barter—the way men traded back in the beginning of history before money was invented. They exchanged goods and services, more like schoolboys trading marbles than like rich men doing business.

It was small wonder that Washington, writing to a friend in 1769, said that unless the British changed their attitude, the Americans, as a last resort, would have to fight for their liberties with arms.

The plight of the Virginia planters was a special case. But nearly everybody—merchants, traders, sailors, farmers and clerks—in all thirteen colonies was hurt, directly or indirectly, by British policy.

In Boston anti-British feeling was probably higher than anywhere else. The richest merchant there was John Hancock, and the new British customs officers who had the job of collecting import duties seemed to be picking on him. Perhaps it was because Hancock was the most important shipper and therefore the best example to all other Boston traders; or perhaps Hancock's troubles with the Customs House arose because he had sided with Sam Adams, who led Boston's public protests against England.

In any case, in June 1768, a party of customs officers seized Hancock's sloop, the *Liberty*.

The news spread through the city in next to no time. And the Boston mob—the gang of men, mostly young, who could be counted on to turn out to protest any British action that in their leaders' opinions deserved condemnation—promptly formed.

That scared the wits out of the customs men. City mobs in the revolutionary period could be terrifying. They almost never had guns, but they did carry clubs, rocks, and cobblestones pried out of the streets.

Along with usually well-behaved, respectable

citizens, the revolutionary mobs included tough, rough characters who sometimes seemed more interested in brawling for its own sake than in whatever political protest was being made. And yet, considering how easily any excited crowd can get out of control, these mobs were well organized and expertly managed. Some of their victims were badly battered—not to mention terrified!—but no one was ever killed, not even accidentally.

At the news that the Boston mob was assembling to attack the customs men for having seized Hancock's sloop, the top customs officials fled to Castle William, a British fort on an island in Boston Harbor.

And as soon as they could recover from their fright, they wrote to England to ask for British soldiers to protect them from the fury of Boston's citizens.

4
Boston: A Massacre and a Tea Party

The British sent troops. Four regiments of red-coated British soldiers arrived in Boston within a few months. This was most unusual because the British had kept very few soldiers in America in spite of all the debate about a 10,000-man army. The citizens of Boston, much as they resented the military occupation, dared not stir up any trouble.

But during the next year, 1769, two regiments left, and the Bostonians grew bolder. When British soldiers walked through the city, people began calling them insulting names like "Lobster!" and "Lobsterback!" Boys threw rocks and snowballs at them and then ducked out of sight. This was less daring than it sounds, because everyone knew that the soldiers had been ordered to avoid trouble at almost any cost.

Yet as time passed these minor incidents became more serious.

Finally, on the cold, snowy night of March 5, 1770, a frightful event took place. The evening had been filled with more than the usual amount of scuffling between citizens and off-duty soldiers, and a false fire alarm had scared everybody. Shortly after nine o'clock, two separate groups of Bostonians—about one hundred men all together —converged on the lone British sentry guarding the Customs House.

An hour or so earlier he had whacked a boy with the butt of his musket for shouting an insult at the captain. Now the guard thought that the mob was going to kill him, for they were shouting: "Kill the soldier! Kill the coward!"

The sentry backed up the Customs House steps, priming his musket as he dodged pieces of wood and chunks of ice that the men in the mob were throwing at him. He yelled for help. Seven more soldiers came running to his aid from the barracks across the square, but the crowd refused to break up.

Captain Preston, the commander of the guard, joined his men and ordered them to prime and load.

"You cowards!" the crowd shouted. "Let's see you fire! You dare not fire! . . . Lobsters! . . . Bloody backs!"

One of the soldiers, hit by something thrown at him, slipped and fell. His musket flew out of his grip. Above the mob's screaming and shouting, the soldiers thought they heard Captain Preston give the order, "Fire!"

They fired. When the smoke cleared, five

Bostonians lay on the snow. Three were dead and two fatally wounded.

In the stunning silence that followed, Preston's guard was quickly reinforced by parts of three companies of soldiers who, on command, dropped to kneeling position, ready to fire. And, as the alarm bells all over Boston rang out, the square filled with hundreds of citizens armed with clubs, knives or anything they had been able to grab. British troops and Boston citizens faced each other in the moonlight. There might have been a terrible slaughter. Luckily Governor Hutchinson and Colonel Dalrymple, commander of all the troops in Boston, arrived and took charge. The soldiers led Preston and his guard away. By three in the morning, the great crowd had dispersed.

It had been murder, Bostonians insisted, ignoring the fact that the mob had provoked the guard. Captain Preston and his men had to be tried.

All the lawyers in Boston were afraid to defend the British soldiers—all, that is, except two. They were John Adams and Josiah Quincy, Jr. Adams was in his middle thirties, learned and hardworking. He was well known as a defender of the rights of Americans, and he was a distant cousin of Sam Adams, the expert politician and leader of the Boston Sons of Liberty, the most active opponents of British rule.

John Adams thought that Great Britain had been wrong in sending troops to Boston. But he also believed that every man is entitled to a fair trial.

Adams and Quincy therefore took the soldiers' case, went over the evidence carefully, and made the jury realize that Captain Preston's guard had acted in self-defense. The court freed all the men. Though the incident is still called the "massacre," most Bostonians—even at the time—realized that the shooting had taken place because the crowd had gotten out of hand.

After the massacre, the British withdrew the rest of their troops from Boston. Soon news came that Parliament, realizing that the customs officers couldn't collect the Townshend duties, had repealed them all except for the tax on tea. England was feeling the effects of the American boycott. Neither side had completely won its point, but both were tired of quarreling. By the fall of 1770, the boycott was ended. Except for English tea, which they still refused to drink, the colonists went back to buying British goods. For two years England and America got along quite well.

Unfortunately, the two-year truce couldn't last. Too many basic disagreements remained, especially the argument over self-rule. The King and his ministers were blind in not understanding that the colonies, every time they kicked up a fuss over British taxes, were as interested in liberty as in money—perhaps more so.

In 1772 there was trouble again. The place was

Massachusetts once more. The conflict was over who should pay Massachusetts' governor. The British government had arranged to pay him, and not to let the Massachusetts Assembly do so.

Since the King appointed the governor, you might think that Massachusetts would have been delighted to have Britain pay his salary and save the money. But the Massachusetts legislators had been able to withhold the governor's salary if he did anything they disliked. That control—which was all they had—was worth much more to Massachusetts voters than the money.

The deed was done, however. For the time being there seemed to be no way for Massachusetts to recover the power she had lost. The citizens of the colony swallowed their defeat, but they started a network of letter writers in all their towns, called Committees of Correspondence. Sam Adams directed the organization of these committees. As the Revolution progressed, their importance grew. They wrote each other news, gave each other advice and in 1773 the network spread to all the colonies. Committees of Correspondence were meeting everywhere and discussing the misdeeds of Parliament, the King, or his latest prime minister, Lord North.

North had become prime minister in 1770. Because he lasted all through the Revolutionary War, Americans came to imagine him as a villain. That was unfair. North was a fat, good-natured man who often fell asleep during Parliamentary debates. When he awoke and found everybody laughing at him, he laughed with them at himself. North was clumsy rather than evil, but he was not the right man to run a government for Americans. "I can never acquiesce," North once said, "in the absurd opinion that all men are created equal."

It wasn't long before North gave the Committees of Correspondence something else to write angry letters about.

The British East India Company was losing money, partly because Americans wouldn't buy its tea. Lord North thought he could help the Company, and his scheme was legalized in the Tea Act of May 1773. Before that law was passed, the East India Company had to sell its tea to English wholesalers, who then sold it to American wholesalers, who sold it to shopkeepers, who sold it to the public—or would have, if the public hadn't refused to buy. The Tea Act allowed the East India Company to cut out both sets of wholesalers. It could ship directly to American agents with exclusive rights to sell tea to Americans. So much money could be saved by eliminating the middlemen that, even including the Townshend tax of three pennies per pound, tea would be cheaper than it had ever been.

King George, Lord North and Parliament were

sure the Americans couldn't resist the marvelous tea bargain.

As usual, they were wrong.

Not only could Americans resist the bargain, but they were outraged. American merchants objected to the monopoly given the tea agents. If Great Britain could establish exclusive rights to sell tea, what was to prevent her from doing the same for all kinds of goods and driving all American importers out of business? Patriots objected because they were as furious as ever about the Townshend tax. The Committees of Correspondence passed the strategy of resistance along: good Americans in every port should go down to the wharves and prevent the East India Company's tea from being landed.

It worked like magic. In New York City, for instance, nearly two thousand men went down to the docks and saw that no tea was landed.

Boston was the only port where difficulty arose. Governor Hutchinson was determined that the East India Company's tea should be unloaded. The Bostonians were just as determined that it should not. The Governor then said that unless the tea ships were unloaded he wouldn't allow them to leave the harbor.

On the night of December 16, 1773, a large crowd of Boston citizens assembled. They had appealed to Governor Hutchinson—a last appeal

—to send the ships, still loaded with tea, back to England.

Word came that the governor refused.

The "Tea Party" that followed was really a masquerade. One hundred and fifty Bostonians wrapped themselves in blankets and daubed red paint and soot on their faces to disguise themselves as Mohawk Indians (and hide their identities from the British authorities). Then they marched down to Griffin's Wharf, where the three tea ships were tied up. They boarded the ships, broke into their holds, hoisted and split apart the chests of tea, and dumped the loose tea leaves into the waters of the harbor.

Thousands of Bostonians stood quietly on the dock, watching. Ships of the British navy rode at anchor only a few hundred yards away. The crowd half expected that the party would be broken up at any moment by gunfire.

Surprisingly, nothing happened.

Admiral Montague, commanding the British ships, happened to be spending the night in a house at the head of Griffin's Wharf. He saw the whole thing. But the admiral did nothing until the tea was all dumped and the "Indians" were marching back toward the center of town.

Then he opened a window and called, "Well, boys. You have had a fine pleasant evening, haven't you? But mind, you'll have to pay the fiddler yet."

One of the young men answered back with a threat. "We'll settle the bill, Squire!" he shouted. "Come down here and we'll settle in two minutes!"

The admiral hastily shut the window.

The next day Boston was singing a song that began:

Rally, Mohawks! Bring out your axes
And tell King George we'll pay no more taxes
On his foreign tea. . . .

And Paul Revere, who had been among the tea dumpers himself, rode off to New York and Philadelphia with a report written by the Boston Committee of Correspondence about the tea party.

Admiral Montague's warning had contained some serious truth, and when Boston heard Parliament's reaction to the affair, scarcely anyone felt like singing.

The port of Boston was closed, starting June 1, 1774, to *all* commerce until the city paid for the tea, which had been worth tens of thousands of dollars.

That would mean that almost everybody in town who worked for a living would be unemployed. Even Governor Hutchinson was shocked at such drastic punishment.

Closing the port was by no means all. Parliament also rewrote part of Massachusetts' charter, making its government even less responsive to the voters' wishes. And for the time being Massachusetts was to have a new governor, General Thomas Gage, British commander-in-chief in North America. Gage would bring soldiers to enforce the new laws.

Parliament at this time also passed the Quebec Act, setting up a government for Canada (eleven years after Great Britain had conquered the country). This Act made the colonists shudder. The Canadians were not to elect any part of their government. To Americans, who were more and more sure that some degree of self-rule was essential, the Quebec Act seemed a terrible example of how their British rulers were thinking.

King George and his Parliament had displayed their power in a frightening way, but the colonists didn't seem to scare easily. They were angry rather than overawed. The punishments aimed at Boston and Massachusetts, moreover, were resented by all the other colonies.

What, if anything, could be done to help Massachusetts? No one was sure, but everybody agreed that a conference was needed.

The busy network of Committees of Correspondence called for a congress of the leaders of the colonies. It would be held in Philadelphia, the largest of American cities, in September 1774. It would try to figure out a peaceful solution for the long list of problems that had arisen between Great Britain and her colonies.

✌ 5
The First Continental Congress

That first Continental Congress faced a bewildering job. Could the delegates agree on recommendations that all Americans would support?

The Congress had to make up its own rules as it went along. The colonies had no legal blueprint, no constitution to serve as a guide. There were no formal political parties. Perhaps the most difficult part of all was the delegates' lack of practical experience—especially in the matter of disagreement between colonies. We now expect our senators and representatives to disagree during a debate but to cooperate with the majority view after a vote has shown what it is. In 1774 there was no such tradition.

Great Britain was a powerful opponent. It seemed obvious that the colonies needed to stand together. "Join or die" was the motto. But how, since practically everyone had a different idea about what should be done, could unity be achieved? What if one, or worse, several of the colonies disagreed?

The meeting had barely started when two shocking pieces of news arrived. First, a war scare. Philadelphia heard the false rumor that British soldiers, commanded by General Gage, had fired on Americans at Boston. The truth was that the British had discovered and taken away a store of five hundred pounds of American gunpowder, but without firing a shot. Before the facts were known, this "Powder Alarm" spread like wildfire throughout the northeastern colonies. Nearly 4,000 Americans marched as far as Cambridge, just outside Boston, where they discovered that the war hadn't really begun.

That fright was barely over before Paul Revere arrived in Philadelphia with real, and ominous, news. Gage was collecting cannons. The British were fortifying the city of Boston. It looked as if Gage was getting ready for war.

In the face of these gathering storm clouds, the Continental Congress reached several bold agreements.

The delegates endorsed a set of resolutions that had just been passed by the Massachusetts voters in Suffolk County. (Paul Revere had brought a copy.) The Suffolk Resolves said that nobody need obey the Boston Port Act and that Americans should begin preparing for a war in case of British attack.

In addition, the Continental Congress voted to renew the American boycott of British goods. This time the boycott was called "The Association," and it was to have a new system of enforcement. Instead of merely asking people not to buy English goods, special Committees of Inspection were to be elected in every town and in every county to see that the Association was observed.

Scarcely any of the delegates could have foreseen the importance of these local committees: they were the seeds of a new government.

For as time went by, these elected committees gathered more and more power. It was quite simple. Americans were willing to obey the decisions of the men—their friends and neighbors—who had been picked in local elections.

The Committees of Inspection immediately took over the job the Committees of Correspondence had been doing. (In many cases the volunteer letter writers were among those elected to the new committees.) And in each colony, if the governor and the old Assembly failed to do what the people wanted, the citizens began to expect their committees to take whatever action was required. Finally the committees grew so important that they could form new governments in each colony and forget about the old.

The situation was unusual among revolutions, because there was never a period of time in which Americans felt they had *no* government at all. There was no lawless reign of terror and anarchy.

Instead, the Americans had two governments —and two loyalties—which overlapped. And gradually they switched from obeying the old to obeying the new.

The first Continental Congress had been very brave about defying King George, Lord North and Parliament. Those delegates who were ready to risk anything rather than back down before Great Britain were delighted.

Others were more cautious. Many of the delegates, along with many Americans in all the colonies, were anxious to try to reason with the British. If the American case could be expressed clearly and fairly, they believed King George would surely come to his senses.

In appreciation of that point of view, the Congress wrote a respectful appeal to the King, and another to the English people. Congress also passed a Declaration of Rights, partly foreshadowing the Declaration of Independence that the next Congress was going to adopt. But the Declaration of Rights merely explained how, in America's opinion, Parliament had violated the colonists' liberties. Congress had no thought of separating from Great Britain, and all these appeals and declarations stressed the colonies' loyalty to the King. Congress adjourned in October, having agreed to meet again in May 1775, if the quarrels weren't settled in the meantime.

Most Americans still believed that Parliament

and Lord North—but *not* King George—were to blame for the trouble. They were wrong. The delegates did not realize that George III had made up his mind, and that appeals to him were a waste of time. In September, while the first Continental Congress was starting its session, the King had already written to Lord North: "The die is cast. . . . The colonies must either submit or triumph."

Many Englishmen thought their stubborn King was wrong. The Americans had supporters—a minority, unfortunately—within Parliament itself.

George III couldn't have cared less.

"I wish nothing but good," he once wrote, "therefore everyone who does not agree with me is a traitor and scoundrel."

✬ 6
Lexington and Concord

General Gage was a mild, moderate man whose wife was American. He had seized the Americans' gunpowder because it was his duty as a British officer to make sure that rebels were in no position to resist the British government. He hoped there would be no trouble, but when his spies reported that the Americans had stores of arms and ammunition at Concord, about eighteen miles from Boston, Gage knew it was his duty to take those weapons away.

The General wanted to surprise Concord, but it was impossible for the British army in Boston to keep secrets. Because the port was closed, the city was full of Bostonians with no jobs who had time to watch every move the British made and report it to the Boston Committee.

On the night of April 18, 1775, Dr. Joseph Warren, head of the Boston Committee, sent for his two best express riders, William Dawes and Paul Revere. He told them the British were sending out troops that night. The redcoats were to march to Lexington to arrest John Hancock and Sam Adams, who were staying there. Then they were to go on to Concord to seize the Americans' stock of weapons. The riders had to get a warning through the circle of British roadblocks around Boston.

Dawes galloped off on one road and slipped past the British sentries in the dark by falling in with some soldiers who happened to be passing the guard post. Revere, after telling an associate to set two signal lanterns in the steeple of the Old North Church, was rowed quietly across the river to Charlestown. There, friends who had seen the lights were waiting with a horse, and away he galloped.

Revere, who had the shorter road, got to Lexington first. Adams and Hancock were bundled off to safety, and the Lexington militia, about 130 men commanded by Captain Jonas Parker, turned out on the village green.

It was four-thirty in the morning before the British appeared. By then nearly half of Parker's men had gone home. The rest—perhaps 70 men in all—formed two lines on the green. They watched, dismayed, while the advance guard of more than 600 British soldiers, in brilliant red and white with gleaming brass buttons and buckles, moved on the double from their column of march into a battle line.

"Stand your ground!" Captain Parker shouted.

THE SIGNAL LANTERNS OF
PAUL REVERE
DISPLAYED IN THE STEEPLE OF THIS CHURCH
APRIL 18 1775
WARNED THE COUNTRY OF THE MARCH
OF THE BRITISH TROOPS TO
LEXINGTON AND CONCORD.

Old North Church, Boston, Massachusetts. Paul Revere's signal lanterns were displayed in the steeple of this church.

"Don't fire unless fired upon. But if they want to have a war, let it begin here!"

And here it began.

Captain Parker, after a moment, realized the hopeless position of his tiny force. Knowing that Adams and Hancock were already safe, he ordered his men to disband.

But the British commander, Major Pitcairn, had orders to disarm the Americans, and he wanted their guns.

"Lay down your arms, you rebels!" the major shouted.

There was a single shot, then an order to fire given by some British officer—not Major Pitcairn —and a platoon volley over the heads of the Americans. A second British volley killed Captain Parker. Before the fight ended—if the few scattered shots returned by the Lexington men could be called a fight—seven other Americans were killed and ten more were wounded.

As the sun rose, the British marched on to Concord. The men of the town had worked all night hiding the military stores from the British. Now they waited in front of Concord for the soldiers to come.

Seeing the overwhelming size of the British column, however, the 150 local militiamen beat a retreat. They withdrew through their town, across North Bridge, a small farm bridge over the

Concord River, and took posts on high ground beyond it.

The British spent the morning searching, with little success, for the hidden guns and ammunition. They accidentally set fire to the courthouse and a blacksmith shop, but quickly put out the flames.

Meanwhile help for the Concord militia was on the way. Every town nearby had heard the church bells ringing an alarm, and militiamen, hurrying to pick up their muskets, formed into squads and marched to the scene. By the time the smoke rose from the fires in Concord, three or four hundred Americans, including reinforcements from Acton, Bedford and Lincoln, were there.

The Americans, thinking the British were burning Concord, decided to reenter the town "or die in the attempt." For two or three minutes the British and the militiamen fired at each other across the North Bridge, and several men on both sides were killed.

The British retreated into Concord and got ready to march back to Boston. The Americans, strengthened every few minutes by the arrival of a new company of militia, prepared to fight a strange battle, a series of flank attacks and ambushes on the British column as it marched along the road. It was a nightmare for the redcoats, drilled to fight in formal formations. The Americans, who fired on the marchers and then hurried ahead to take up new positions and fire again, seemed to be everywhere; flashes of musket fire blazed at the British from houses, barns, from behind stone walls and trees. British casualties were heavy.

By the time the British column reached Lexington, the running fight had turned into a rout. The redcoats were badly disorganized. If the Americans had been an army instead of small volunteer units rushing to the scene of action, the British force might have been wiped out.

But a British rescue party of 1,000 soldiers was on the way. General Gage had guessed that, in spite of his hopes, there might be trouble for his expedition. And though the Americans continued to attack along the entire sixteen-mile route back to Boston, especially near the towns of Arlington and Cambridge, the fresh body of British troops with additional artillery prevented the defeat from being worse than it was. The British lost 273 men either killed, wounded or missing—more than twice as many as the Americans.

As the British force reached the safety of Boston after sunset, a ring of Massachusetts militiamen closed in around the city. In a matter of days, militiamen from all the neighboring colonies marched in to join the Massachusetts men. Ten thousand recruits surrounded Boston, blockading it from the land—just as the British had blockaded it by sea.

❧ 7
Bunker's Hill

On June 15, 1775, the second Continental Congress, which had met as planned on May 10th, chose a general "to command all the continental forces raised, or to be raised, for the defense of American liberty."

The man it picked was 43-year-old George Washington, a delegate from Virginia who had fought in the French and Indian War—a man with a good deal of army experience, but primarily a civilian. And yet, as those who knew him agreed, the Virginia planter who had served in his colony's assembly and had also represented Virginia in the first Continental Congress was a man of great character and determination. Everyone hoped that Washington's personal qualities might make up for his lack of experience in running an army.

General Washington rode from Philadelphia to take command of the troops outside Boston, who had another taste of action before he arrived.

In those days, Boston was a city of less than twenty thousand. North of it, on a peninsula between the Mystic and the Charles rivers, lay the town of Charlestown—now part of Boston. And on Charlestown Neck, as that peninsula was called, were Bunker's Hill and Breed's Hill. American cannons placed on those hills could bombard Boston.

One of the American generals already on the scene was peppery old Israel Putnam of Connecticut, a hero of the French and Indian War. He strongly favored fortifying the hills because he thought a bombardment of Boston from Charlestown Neck might force the British to leave the city. Putnam's superior, General Artemas Ward of Massachusetts, who commanded the Americans before Washington's arrival, listened to Putnam's arguments despite his own fears over the American gunpowder shortage. There were only eleven barrels of powder in the entire American camp.

Despite the danger that the Americans might provoke the well-supplied British into an attack, 1,200 militiamen commanded by Colonel William Prescott of Massachusetts marched from Cambridge to Charlestown Neck on the night of June 16th. Putnam joined the marchers. Although the plan was to fortify Bunker's Hill, the officers decided to build the main base on Breed's Hill first, because it was closer to Boston, and then dig in on Bunker's. The work began around midnight, only four hours before the dawn that would expose the Americans to the British.

The eastern sky lightened. A sharp-eyed lookout on one of the British warships in the Charles River spotted the American stronghold, and the ship's captain opened fire. A few hours later several other men-of-war and a British gun battery on Copp's Hill in Boston all were shelling the American position. Their firing reached a climax around noon. Then the Americans saw what they most feared. Fifteen hundred redcoats with brass cannons, gleaming steel bayonets and full field equipment were loaded onto small boats and ferried across toward Charlestown Neck, ready to attack. General William Howe, who would soon replace Gage as the British army's commander-in-chief, led the expedition.

The day—June 17th—was dreadfully hot. The Americans, who had marched and dug the whole night long, were tired and hungry and, to complete their misery, they had run out of water.

Meanwhile some American reinforcements were moving onto the peninsula. The largest group was John Stark's New Hampshire detachment. But they were very short of gunpowder, and had only about fifteen bullets apiece. These they had just made for themselves out of the lead pipes of an organ in a Cambridge church.

Howe's men landed easily, but storming the

hastily prepared American line—made up of the new stronghold, a breastwork, a rail fence and a stone wall—was another matter. Despite their superiority in numbers, weapons, training and leadership, the British still had to attack, mostly uphill. The ground was rough, and each British infantryman carried more than a hundred pounds of equipment.

The British, trying to get into position for a final bayonet charge, moved slowly forward in two brilliant scarlet lines. The Americans, behind their improvised fortifications, had been ordered not to fire until the enemy was so close that they could see the whites of their eyes. Ammunition was so scarce that they dared not waste a single shot.

Just as Howe's men got to the point where the bayonet charge should have begun, the blast of musket fire from the Americans shattered their lines. Every man on General Howe's personal staff was killed or wounded. The British fell back.

Fifteen minutes after the failure of the first assault, the British tried again. This time the American lines were completely silent until the enemy had approached to within one hundred feet. Then they fired again—a blast even more devastating than the first—and kept on firing, loading and reloading as fast as they could, for nearly half an hour. All that time, though men were dropping like flies, the brave British tried to keep on.

Some companies lost three-quarters or nine-tenths of their men within minutes. Finally the British retreated.

There was a long wait, and then a third British assault, a bayonet charge. So far American losses had been light, but their ammunition was almost gone, and they had no bayonets to meet the British steel. Even so, many of the Massachusetts, Connecticut and New Hampshire men stayed in their positions though all they could do was use their muskets as clubs. And the American retreat, when Prescott ordered it, was an orderly movement, not a flight.

The British captured Breed's Hill, Bunker's Hill and all of Charlestown Neck at a terrible cost. Almost half the 2,400 British soldiers who took part were wounded, and 226—including Major Pitcairn, whose troops had fired on the Lexington militia—were killed. American losses—140 killed, 270 wounded, 30 taken prisoner—were lighter, but heavy enough to shock all the colonies into realizing what war with Britain was likely to mean.

The battle has always been called Bunker's Hill even though Breed's Hill was where the little stronghold stood. The fighting was a foretaste of something the war would prove: that both British and American soldiers were capable of great bravery. Americans had thought the redcoats were not "free men," and therefore cowards. The

British had thought that Americans, lacking military discipline, could never stand up against a professional army's attack.

Neither idea—as both sides would continue to find, to their sorrow—was correct.

❧ 8

The Americans Attack Canada

When the Continental Congress made General Washington commander-in-chief, it also appointed several other generals. One of them was Philip Schuyler of New York. He was ordered to Albany, his hometown, to command two forts on Lake Champlain—Ticonderoga and Crown Point. Both forts had just been captured from the British by a force of Connecticut and Vermont men (Vermont was then part of New York) called Green Mountain Boys, led by Ethan Allen.

These two forts were key positions on the water route to Canada. Once they were in American hands, it was logical to think of a military expedition into British-held Canada which might bring the Canadians into the war on the American side. About two thousand English-speaking people lived in Canada, many of them known to be pro-American. The French-speaking Canadians were more of a question, but Congress hoped that they, too, would join the American troops.

As the expedition's commander, General

Schuyler stayed close to Albany to manage the tremendous supply job. The actual fighting force was led by General Richard Montgomery, a charming 39-year-old, who had been a captain in the British army before he resigned to live in Dutchess County, New York, and marry a New York girl.

Montgomery's troops included Connecticut men and some Green Mountain Boys, but four New York regiments were the heart of his command. At first Montgomery had had doubts about the "Yorkers." Many of their officers had been leaders of the New York mob, and many of the soldiers were the poorest of the poor. But as the fighting progressed, they proved their worth.

On November 13th the Americans scrambled into Montreal, having captured a string of British forts on their way. General Guy Carleton, the British governor of Canada, escaped two days before Montreal surrendered. He traveled 150 miles down the St. Lawrence River and prepared to defend the fortress-city Quebec—built on rocky heights above the river—against American siege.

Meanwhile, a second American expeditionary force, six hundred soldiers commanded by Colonel Benedict Arnold, had arrived outside Quebec. It had started from Cambridge, Massachusetts, forty-five days earlier, with almost twice that many men. They had marched through the Maine

Fort Ticonderoga, New York. The stronghold on the southern end of Lake Champlain, near the outlet from Lake George, commanded this junction on the water route from New York City to Montreal. The south wall of the interior fort is in the shape of a hollow square. The Americans captured Ticonderoga from the British, lost it when Burgoyne invaded from Canada and reoccupied it just before Burgoyne's defeat at Saratoga, New York.

woods when the rains, flooding and snow were at their worst. But Arnold had kept his men moving forward even after they had run out of food and some were trying to eat shoe leather. When they arrived on the banks of the St. Lawrence, opposite Quebec, the men looked more like scarecrows than soldiers. Still, their feat was magnificent and their march is one of the greatest in the history of war.

On December 2nd, Montgomery's troops —three hundred men, with artillery, clothing and provisions—joined Arnold's. Together the two American forces took up positions below Quebec. The Americans had no time to waste. The Canadians refused to provide food or ammunition except for money, and wouldn't accept the only money Montgomery had, paper money issued by the Continental Congress. Furthermore, the enlistments of most of Arnold's troops expired on the last day of the month, and there was no hope of keeping the men after that. A long, drawn-out siege of Quebec was impossible.

Montgomery and Arnold decided to try a brave but desperate move—to storm the walls of Quebec on the first dark, snowy night.

Knowing the danger, one young captain on Montgomery's staff, Joseph Cheeseman, put some gold coins in his pocket as he dressed for the battle, saying that they would pay for his burial.

Unfortunately, he was right. Everything went wrong that cold night, the last night of 1775. In

The Citadel, Quebec, Canada. The fortress on the St. Lawrence River was a position too tough for the Americans, under General Montgomery and Colonel Arnold, to take by storm.

the first attack, both Cheeseman and his commander, Montgomery, were killed. Arnold fell, wounded in the leg, and had to be carried to the rear. Daniel Morgan, captain of the Virginia riflemen; John Lamb, New York's artillery commander; and 424 other officers and men were taken prisoner.

By morning—and New Year's Day, 1776— the British and General Carleton had won an overwhelming victory.

For a long time, Colonel Arnold hoped that Congress would send reinforcements and the Americans could try again. But by the time the soldiers arrived, Carleton also had been reinforced. Then smallpox, a terrible foe, swept through the American army. Finally the Americans could do nothing but retreat, following the same route Montgomery had taken on his way north, fighting off the British pursuers as they went. In July 1776, those Americans who had survived were back where they had started from, the forts at Crown Point and Ticonderoga.

❧ 9
The British Leave Boston and the Americans Declare Their Independence

Some of the sting was taken out of Montgomery's defeat at Quebec by an American triumph at Boston. The British were forced to leave the city.

That had been General Washington's objective from the moment he had taken command. But at first, the gunpowder shortage which had crippled the American attempt to hold Breed's Hill had made an attack against Boston impractical. Washington also had been faced with the problem that plagued Arnold at Quebec—his troops' enlistments all expired the last day of December 1775. The militiamen who answered the alarms after the Lexington skirmish were private citizens who, as part-time soldiers, did not expect to serve for long. Their military training was skimpy. They elected their own officers, and often felt entirely free to disobey them. And although Congress had started to raise Continental regiments designed to serve as a regular American army, it had begun by asking for enlistments of only one year. It supposed the war would be short.

General Washington begged his militiamen to stay with him for just a few days beyond the end of December until new recruits arrived. Some stayed. Others simply walked out of camp and headed home, taking their irreplaceable muskets with them. If the British had known how few men there were in the American lines around Boston at the beginning of January 1776, they might have strolled out of the city with ease.

Besides powder, guns and men, Washington's army lacked artillery—cannons big enough to do some damage at long range. But at least Washington knew where there were such guns—at Ticonderoga and Crown Point. Washington sent his 25-year-old artillery officer, Colonel Henry Knox, to get them.

Before the war ended, Knox was in command of all the American artillery. But he began as a huge, jolly, enthusiastic amateur whose hobby was guns. Although he had been a member of a Boston militia artillery company, bookselling was his job. He kept a bookstore, and he had learned about military science by reading all books on the subject before he sold them.

Getting the guns from Lake Champlain to Boston was an amazing achievement. There were about fifty of the great things. Knox had heavy sleds built to carry them and found eighty pairs of oxen to drag them overland. The Berkshire Hills in western Massachusetts, deep in winter snow, were a serious obstacle. Knox got horses to help the oxen, and struggled through the drifts with his precious cargo.

He delivered the guns in February, and then Washington—although two thousand of his nine thousand soldiers had no muskets—saw a way of making Boston too hot for the British.

There were hills named Dorchester Heights south of the city. As cannon sites, these were about as good as Bunker's and Breed's hills. For two nights—March 2nd and March 3rd—Washington's soldiers in the lines on the western side of Boston kept up a heavy display of fire from dusk until dawn, spending gunpowder as they had never spent it before. They were concealing the really important work in progress.

More than two thousand men, under cover of the smoke and racket, were hauling cannons to Dorchester Heights, putting them in place and digging fortifications to protect both the guns and the gunners.

The British were taken by surprise. On the morning of March 4th, General Howe saw the results of the Americans' enterprise through a spyglass. "The rebels have done more in one night than my whole army could do in months," he said. Of course he didn't realize it had really taken the rebels *two* nights.

Howe was furious. The American guns on

Dorchester Heights not only commanded Boston, threatening the British army there, but made the Boston harbor unsafe for the ships of the British navy. Howe immediately planned an attack to win the Heights back, but then he decided it was wiser to abandon Boston altogether. A bad storm blew up, and he used it as his official excuse for not striking back.

Howe loaded his soldiers onto troop transports and warships, taking with him more than a thousand Massachusetts Tories—pro-British Americans who preferred exile to staying behind with their rebellious countrymen—and sailed away.

On March 17, 1776, the American army marched proudly back into Boston. For the time being there was no British army in the thirteen colonies.

The following month, April, the Continental Congress at Philadelphia took a big step toward American independence. It announced that American ports were open to ships of all nations *except* Great Britain. That was only a gesture. British men-of-war had blockaded the ports since the summer of 1775. The Americans, who had practically no navy, had no power to get French or Dutch or Spanish vessels past those British watchdogs. Still, the gesture was important. For the

Culver Service

The Craigie-Longfellow House, Cambridge, Massachusetts.
This residence served as American army headquarters
during the siege of Boston.

first time, Americans denied the King's right to control their foreign trade.

In May the Congress took another revolutionary step. It recommended that the colonies form new governments if they hadn't already done so. The old governments had collapsed. Most of the governors had fled, yet each colony needed someone to do the governor's job. Something more formal than government by committees was needed. Naturally the new governments were to have no connection at all with Parliament or with the King of England.

As each of these steps toward independence was considered, it stirred up heated debates—not only in the Continental Congress, but among Americans everywhere. In January 1776, a pamphlet called *Common Sense,* written by Tom Paine, was published. It was a best seller, and it argued boldly for independence—in sometimes shocking language, as when it called George III "a royal brute."

Paine's arguments helped many Americans decide that a complete break with Great Britain was the right solution. Yet others still would have been happy to remain part of the British Empire if only George III had shown any willingness to meet the Americans halfway.

Most Americans agreed that the British in England lived under the best government in the world. Their Parliament had the last word.

English subjects could not be sent to jail on a mere administrator's order, like French subjects. Only if they had been found guilty by a jury could they be imprisoned. Englishmen were not taxed without their consent. The great trouble was that Americans were not being treated like Englishmen. And if they were not to have the rights of Englishmen, more and more Americans thought they had better fight for the rights of Americans.

In England, three thousand miles away, the Americans' complaints seemed strange. The majority of Englishmen thought that agitators and troublemakers had stirred up the city mobs and that the revolutionary leaders did not fully represent the American people. That is what King George believed. He also imagined that by smashing the rebellion quickly, he would bring the colonists to their senses and make them loyal subjects again.

In May, Virginia took the lead by instructing her delegates in the Continental Congress to ask for a declaration of independence. On June 7th Richard Henry Lee, a Virginia delegate, moved:

That these United Colonies are, and of right ought to be, free and independent States: that they are absolved from all allegiance to the British Crown; and that all political connection between them and the State of Great Britain is, and ought to be, totally dissolved.

Because many delegates were not yet ready to take this final step, the Congress postponed the debate on Lee's motion for three weeks. In the meantime, a five-man committee started to draft a longer declaration to have ready in case the Congress wanted one. One of the committee's members was a talented young redhead from Virginia, Thomas Jefferson. His fellow committeemen felt that he was the best writer among them and should therefore do the actual writing. Jefferson's many abilities were to lead him to the White House as the third President of the United States, and the declaration he wrote is one of the United States' most famous and inspiring pieces of writing.

But before it could be published, the Continental Congress had to adopt it. They debated independence on July 1st and voted for it on July 2nd. The delegates then went over Jefferson's text, sentence by sentence, made some changes and on July 4th adopted it in the form we know.

John Adams, another member of the drafting committee, wrote his wife, who was at their home in Massachusetts:

The second day of July, 1776, will be the most memorable . . . in the history of America. I . . . believe that it will be celebrated by succeeding generations as the great anniversary festival . . . with shows, games, sports, balls,

61

bonfires, and illuminations, from one end of this continent to the other, from this time forward forever more.

Except for the date—for we celebrate the day on which the Congress approved the final wording of the Declaration, July 4th—John Adams was a wonderful prophet.

❧ 10
Washington Loses,
Crosses the Delaware and Wins

From Boston General Howe had sailed to Halifax, Nova Scotia. There thousands of new soldiers joined his army, including German troops hired by King George from various German princes. Americans called all the German soldiers "Hessians," and some, but by no means all, actually came from Hesse in Germany.

Howe's complete force—more than 30,000 soldiers and a huge navy—was the largest expeditionary force that the British had ever assembled.

The question was, where would that force strike?

General Washington felt almost sure that New York City was Howe's objective. So did the New Yorkers who, after a slow start, were working hard to fortify their town.

They were right. New York had been the British army headquarters in the past, and geographically it was more important than Boston. It stood at the mouth of the Hudson River, which led almost to Lake George and Lake Champlain, which were connected by rivers to the St. Lawrence. The British grand strategy was to capture that water route to Canada—the route Montgomery had taken in 1775—thereby cutting off the New England colonies and dividing the Americans in two.

On August 22nd, Howe opened his assault on New York City by landing in Brooklyn. Brooklyn Heights, across the East River from the small town on the southern tip of Manhattan Island, was the key to the military problem.

The battle was hardly a contest. The English outnumbered the Americans by more than two to one, and the American generals, John Sullivan and Israel Putnam, last-minute replacements for General Nathanael Greene, who was sick, were unfamiliar with the battlefield. Three Long Island Tories led one of Howe's columns through an important pass which the Americans, carelessly, were guarding with only five men. Before the Americans knew what had happened, part of Howe's army was around one flank, and the redcoats were moving at them from two different directions at once. There was nothing for the Americans to do except fall back to their fortifications on Brooklyn Heights.

It was a disaster. The Americans lost more than a thousand men—most of them taken prisoner—by bad generalship. Luckily General Howe, who so far had managed his troops almost perfectly, made the next mistake. Instead of letting his soldiers fight on, elated as they were by their victory, Howe halted them in front of the American line of trenches and strongholds.

For two days the Americans waited, expecting the British to attack at any time. Then a bad rainstorm blew in from the northeast, making it impossible for the British men-of-war to sail into the East River and cut off the only possible American escape route—across the river to Manhattan.

General Washington, in his New York headquarters on Manhattan Island, ordered every small boat in the neighborhood collected. The rain continued to pour down. On the night of August 29th, with the storm still blowing furiously, he turned the collection of assorted boats over to the men of two Massachusetts regiments from Marblehead and Salem. All of them had been sailors or fishermen before enlisting. In the teeth of a gale that kept the British navy at anchor, the Massachusetts men rowed the entire American force—9,500 men, with all their equipment, guns, horses and provisions—across the East River to the safety of the New York shore.

The brilliant escape saved half the entire American army, but wars are not won by escaping from the enemy. By losing Brooklyn, Washington had lost the chance of keeping Howe out of New York City—if, indeed, he had ever had it. The

The Morris-Jumel Mansion, New York City. Washington moved here on September 14, 1776, to direct his unsuccessful attempt to keep Manhattan Island out of British hands.

British navy, unopposed, could sail almost all around Manhattan Island, except when the weather was foul. Howe could land his soldiers anywhere north of the built-up area and cut off New York City at almost any time he chose.

But the British postponed the attack on New York. Both General Howe and his brother, Admiral Howe, who commanded the British fleet, were dissatisfied with England's American policy. They wanted to make one last attempt at a peaceful settlement.

The Continental Congress appointed three members—Benjamin Franklin, John Adams and Edward Rutledge—to meet the Howe brothers on Staten Island in New York Harbor on September 11th. The conference got nowhere. As peace commissioners, the Howes had been empowered only to pardon rebels who said they were sorry —nothing more. They had no terms to offer. From the Americans' point of view there was nothing to discuss, much less accept.

That left it up to the Howe brothers to continue with the King's plan—to give the American army a thorough licking.

On September 15th the British attacked across the East River in specially built assault boats. They landed at what is now the foot of East 34th Street, and before dark, New York City was theirs. The Americans fled in panic to high ground at the upper end of Manhattan, named Harlem Heights.

Ottilie Johnson

The Billopp House, Tottenville, Staten Island, New York. Here the Howe brothers, on September 11, 1776, conferred with Franklin, Adams and Rutledge, hoping that peaceful negotiation might still be possible.

The next day the Americans met the British in front of the Heights in a small battle, and for a change it was the British who retreated. Still, Washington realized he had to leave Manhattan because the British controlled the rivers and Long Island Sound and might at any time land behind the Americans and trap them.

Washington retreated north into Westchester County, leaving a considerable garrison in Fort Washington, in northern Manhattan, in the hope that the fort's guns might annoy British warships on the Hudson River.

The British followed Washington. The battle of White Plains (October 28, 1776) was a British victory, but not a decisive one. After it, Howe showed no desire to chase Washington and try for a knockout blow; he took his troops back to Manhattan. Meanwhile—except for the troops in Fort Washington—the Americans were crossing the Hudson into New Jersey.

On November 14th, in a skillful, many-pronged attack, the British captured Fort Washington. It was a tragic loss for the Americans. Some of Washington's finest troops had been lost on a hopeless idea. In addition to 150 men killed or wounded, more than 2,800 Americans were taken prisoner. And the prisoners who were enlisted men—although not the 230 officers— were treated with horrible cruelty in the months to come. They were locked up in overcrowded warehouses, substitutes for jails, where they died of disease, hunger and maltreatment. The name of William Cunningham, the British provost marshal in charge of prisoners, became a symbol for terrifying brutality.

George Washington had lost more than the garrison of a fort. For a time, at least, he had lost the public confidence. People whispered that he couldn't make up his mind; that he depended too much on congressional approval; that he put too much faith in General Greene's advice—because Greene had favored the attempt to hold Fort Washington.

Among the loudest whisperers was the second-ranking American general, Charles Lee, who had impressed the delegates to the Congress—Washington included—by exaggerating his experience as an English army officer. Lee had hopes of replacing Washington. As Washington continued to retreat across New Jersey, he ordered Lee and his 5,000 men, who were still on the east side of the Hudson north of White Plains, to join him. But Lee took inexcusably long to obey. When he finally started, Lee marched at the snail's pace of three miles a day. He was surprised by the British in a tavern just south of Morristown, New Jersey, and taken prisoner. Less than half his men reached the main American camp.

By the middle of December 1776, General Washington's army—no more than 6,000 men

—had retreated to the west or Pennsylvania side of the Delaware River near Trenton, leaving all northern New Jersey in British hands. The Americans seemed to have no fight left after their series of defeats and withdrawals. General Howe was so confident that he could easily finish off Washington that he sent a large section of the British army to capture Newport, Rhode Island, which was undefended. They were to settle into winter quarters there.

In those days, wars usually stopped during the bad winter weather. The British, with New York and Newport in their hands, decided not to push on to Philadelphia even though it looked as if the city was theirs practically for the taking, since only the discouraged American force stood in the way. But Howe decided to wait until spring. He pulled most of his men back to New York, leaving just a skeleton force in several New Jersey towns to keep an eye on Washington's ragged, war-weary troops.

It crossed Washington's mind that *now*—just when the British assumed that nothing was going to happen—might be the best time for an American counterattack. The general planned to divide his army into three groups, cross the Delaware at three different points in long, low river boats, and then unite them for a nine-mile march and a surprise attack on the Hessians in Trenton. He would use almost every man in his whole army—a desperate risk because Washington had no way of making sure that his soldiers could get back across the water should the attack fail. Washington preferred not to think too much about that dreadful possibility.

The main body of Americans crossed the river after dark on Christmas night. It was bitterly cold. The air was filled with a mixture of sleet and hail. Chunks of ice floating in the Delaware made the passage slow—a serious matter because Washington counted, for surprise, on reaching Trenton before daylight. None of the Americans had winter uniforms. Most of them were wearing worn-out summer civilian clothes, and quite a few were shoeless. They were marching on the icy road, in snow, their feet tied with old rags. They left bloody footprints on the road to Trenton.

At eight o'clock on the morning of the 26th, with almost perfect coordination, the Americans charged into Trenton from both ends of the town. Except for a few guards, most of the Hessians were still in bed recovering from their giant Christmas celebration of feasting and drinking that had lasted until late the previous night. Before they could pull themselves together, the Americans were all over town. By nine o'clock, after an hour of confused hurly-burly, the fighting was over. Trenton, and almost 1,000 Hessian prisoners, belonged to Washington's shabby but triumphant army.

Sauders photo from Cushing

The Old Barracks, Trenton, New Jersey. In 1776 Hessian soldiers slept here after a big Christmas celebration, never dreaming that Washington's small army had crossed the Delaware.

The victory had an electric effect on all Americans. From despair they moved to confidence. Doubts about Washington's ability were completely erased. Congress immediately backed the general to its utmost. And Washington's men, inspired by victory, continued to do him proud.

The Americans attacked again in just a few days. General Charles Cornwallis, with a strong British force, moved south from Princeton planning to retake Trenton. Washington's force was hardly a match for the British in a head-on slugging contest, but again he used surprise to make up for lack of numbers. On the night of January 2, 1777, while a small party of soldiers stayed behind to keep the campfires burning brightly and fool the enemy, Washington marched north. He circled quietly around the British, moving well to the east. Orders were whispered. The wheels of the gun carriages were wrapped with rags to muffle their noise.

By early morning on January 3rd, the Americans were within a mile or two of Princeton, fighting the British rear guard, before Cornwallis knew what had happened. The battle was short and severe. At first the British men had the best of it; a British bayonet charge scattered the Americans in confusion. Then Washington himself, riding his huge white horse, appeared on the scene. The general seemed entirely unaware of danger. He and his aides rode right into the front of the action, shouting encouragement to the American soldiers. Reinforcements arrived. The retreating Americans were finally re-formed; then they advanced, firing as they went. The British retreated, not toward Princeton, but south down the main road toward Trenton.

In the meantime, part of the British rear guard had been driven the other way, back to Princeton. Some of them had gone north on the road to New Brunswick. Another group, 194 men, took refuge in Nassau Hall, then—and now—part of Princeton University. Captain Alexander Hamilton, an American artilleryman, fired one shot into the building. Then a party of New Jersey men entered it and the entire British group was taken prisoner.

Washington had won another small but important victory. But Princeton was no place for his army to stay; Cornwallis had turned around and was hurrying up from Trenton.

If Washington had had a few fresh regiments —just six or seven hundred men, according to his own estimate—he would have headed for New Brunswick, the main British supply depot in New Jersey. But since, on the contrary, all his men were very tired, he marched instead toward the hilly, heavily wooded campsite near Morristown that he had picked out earlier as his base.

Cornwallis, fooled again, hurried to protect New Brunswick, and on January 6th American troops seized control of Hackensack and Elizabeth-

Nassau Hall, Princeton, New Jersey. This building on the grounds of Princeton University was used as a refuge for 194 British soldiers of General Cornwallis' rear guard.

town. That left the British in possession of only Amboy and New Brunswick. All the rest of New Jersey, and control of the state, had been snatched right out of the bewildered British general's hands. It was almost incredible, considering that Washington's counterattack had been fought by only 5,000 men, mostly militia, who lacked everything soldiers should have—except courage and a great leader.

Brandywine and Germantown

Washington settled down in winter camp at Morristown and spent the first five months of 1777 trying to raise a new army, for enlistments had again expired at the end of 1776. Recruiting was dangerously slow. That was partly because so many young men had heard about the horrible conditions in the army, and partly because Continental soldiers were paid late and in Continental paper money, which had been steadily losing value.

The danger was that General Howe, whose big army was in excellent shape, might attack while the Americans were still struggling to sign up a new fighting force.

Curiously, Howe never stirred from New York City. And by May, Washington had assembled 8,000 soldiers, with more to come.

General Howe was, and remains, a puzzle. He was an able officer, and certainly not a coward. No one understood why he moved so slowly. His beautiful battle plans were successful, but Howe hesitated to follow up his victories. Some people thought he was cautious because he had never recovered from the shock of the slaughter on the slopes of Breed's Hill. Others talked about his longstanding lack of enthusiasm for Britain's war against America.

In any case, Howe did nothing until Washington was fairly well reorganized. Then in June the British engaged the Americans at several places in New Jersey, but without any important results. Whereupon Howe withdrew all the British troops to New York City and Staten Island.

What did that mean? What was Howe planning to do next?

Washington knew that "Gentleman Johnny" Burgoyne, the British general who had spent the winter in London persuading King George to let him lead a big expedition down from Quebec along the water route to Albany, was on the move with a force almost as big as the entire American army. It seemed likely that Howe planned to move north, up the Hudson, to meet Burgoyne and cut the American war effort in two.

But Washington thought that Howe was a tricky strategist. Perhaps Philadelphia, or even Charleston, South Carolina, would be Howe's next objective. Therefore, while Washington began to detach a few brigades from his army and order them to march part of the way toward Albany, the general himself waited with most of his troops in

The Ford Mansion, Morristown, New Jersey. In 1777, after the Battle of Princeton, Washington took his army to Morristown for the rest of the winter, and the camp there was an important base from late 1779 to the end of the war. The general used Mrs. Jacob Ford's house as his headquarters.

New Jersey until he could be sure of Howe's plan.

On July 23rd Howe's great fleet of more than 260 warships and troop transports, which carried close to 17,000 soldiers, sailed away from New York and headed out to sea. Washington immediately started his army south in the direction of Philadelphia. However, he knew that Burgoyne had already captured Ticonderoga, and it seemed almost incredible that Howe did not intend to join him. Was Howe's sailing an elaborate ruse? Might he double back—now that Washington had left the Hudson—and take his fleet up the river after all?

The suspense lasted for an entire month. Finally, on August 25th the British began landing on the northern shore of Chesapeake Bay in Maryland. They were headed for Philadelphia, seat of the Continental Congress and the unofficial capital of America. Washington hurried his troops south to try to block the threat. With Washington went a volunteer, a 20-year-old French nobleman, the Marquis de Lafayette, who had come to America to fight for liberty. Washington soon came to love Lafayette as if he were his own son; and Lafayette, whose admiration for the general was boundless, served Washington for the duration of the war.

The Americans marched to Chadd's Ford, a tiny Pennsylvania town at a shallow crossing of Brandywine Creek—about halfway between Philadelphia and the British landing place. Meanwhile the British plowed their way north. The two armies clashed in the fierce battle of the Brandywine on September 11, 1777. The Americans were badly beaten. They lost, as they had lost the Battle of Long Island in Brooklyn, because their knowledge of the ground was poor. There were more places where the Brandywine could be crossed than they realized. They expected the British to attack head on; instead, a column of English troops led by General Cornwallis crossed upstream with some artillery and surprised the American right flank. Washington's men fought hard in brave confusion, but they had been completely outmaneuvered. They were forced from the battlefield, and the entire American army retreated some twelve miles to Chester—halfway from Brandywine Creek to Philadelphia.

The defeat was bitter, but Washington's men were not despairing, nor had they lost their self-respect. However, in Philadelphia the Continental Congress was alarmed—and rightly so—and fled to York, Pennsylvania. On September 26th, after ten days of constant maneuvering and a few skirmishes, the British captured Philadelphia.

Within a day or two, the Americans were itching for a chance to redeem themselves. Howe's main camp was at Germantown, a village just northwest of Philadelphia. There, Washington decided, he would attack.

The Battle of Germantown, on October 3, 1777, started well for the Americans in spite of the fact that Washington's plan was too complex. He had divided his army into four columns which were to march down four different roads, surprise the British and close in on them like the crushing jaws of a giant nutcracker. One of Washington's columns came down the Skippack Road to Philadelphia, tangled with British light infantry and beat them back, although Howe himself rushed to the front to urge his soldiers to hold their ground.

But in the retreat, more than a hundred Britishers slipped into the Chew House, a large stone building beside the road, and started rapid firing on the Americans from the second-story windows. The Americans should have bypassed it and pushed on, but their officers were stronger on book learning than practical military experience. Colonel Knox, the bookseller-turned-artilleryman, had read that an advancing army should never leave an enemy's "fortified castle" behind it. He regarded the house full of Britishers as just that. And so, on Knox's advice, the American column stopped to try to blow the house down with light artillery fire.

Knox's six-pound cannon balls merely bounced off the massive stone walls, and the noise of the

The Chew House, Germantown, Pennsylvania. These walls were much too strong for the six-pound cannon balls of Colonel Henry Knox's artillery on October 3, 1777.

firing in this unexpected place helped to confuse Washington's other columns. The morning was foggy, and gunpowder smoke made it even harder for the Americans to see where they were going. At one mixed-up moment, two American divisions collided. They fired at each other, and then both outfits broke in panic and ran.

One American mistake followed another. By the time the main battle in the village developed, the Americans were exhausted. Many of the soldiers had already used up all their ammunition. The British pushed them back. Finally, Washington's entire force settled into a confused, slow-motion retreat.

The ambitious plan had failed, and the Americans had suffered another defeat. Yet the contest had been much closer than Washington's soldiers realized at the time. "We ran from victory," General "Mad Anthony" Wayne said later. The very idea that the Americans, after so many losses, had dared attempt to pounce on Howe's army was impressive. General Howe, who was among those impressed, pulled back to Philadelphia and began barricading the city against an American attack.

But Washington's army, after its near miss at Germantown, was worn out, barefoot, hungry and in no condition—no matter what Howe thought —to attack Philadelphia. Washington moved his men to Valley Forge, Pennsylvania, for the winter.

❧ 12
The Saratoga Campaign

Bennington

While Howe was moving on Philadelphia, Gentleman Johnny Burgoyne, a red-faced, 55-year-old fashion plate, was making himself unpopular in upstate New York. Burgoyne had had a play produced in London, and greatly admired his own writing ability. He published a long, flowery statement trying to explain his march toward Albany.

But Burgoyne's fancy phrases backfired. Instead of soothing, or even scaring, the Americans, his statement made them furious. The Green Mountain Boys of Vermont came out to fight, joining New Hampshire men who had hurried to enlist.

From Fort Ticonderoga, which he captured, Burgoyne continued south toward Fort Edward on the Hudson River. His troops hacked their way from the southern end of Lake Champlain through 23 swampy miles of giant pines and hemlocks. In his strong, 7,500-man army, Burgoyne had not only British and German regulars but 250 Canadians and 400 Indians. On July 27th, two days before Burgoyne occupied Fort Edward, which General Schuyler had abandoned, a group of Indian scouts committed a shocking murder—and gave American recruiting officers additional anti-Burgoyne fuel to throw on the fire.

The victim's name was Jane McCrea. She was twenty-three and engaged to marry David Jones, a Tory who had fled to Canada to fight for the British. When Burgoyne's Indian scouts found her, Jane was staying with an elderly lady, Mrs. McNeil, near Fort Edward—waiting, she hoped, to meet David. The Indians promised to lead the two ladies to the British. But they had not gone far before one of the Indians quarreled with another Indian over which was Jane's guard. He shot her, scalped her and tore the clothes off her body.

Burgoyne's first thought was to execute the Indian, whose name was Wyandot Panther. But he changed his mind for fear that if he did so, the rest of the Indians would desert. It was a poor decision. Within a short time Burgoyne's Indians deserted anyhow. And thousands of New Englanders, outraged by stories of Jane's unavenged murder, marched toward Albany to reinforce the northern army.

At almost the same time, Burgoyne made another mistake. His German cavalry, dressed in stiff leather trousers and huge cocked hats, had been having a miserable time for an understandable reason—they had no horses. Once the British reached Fort Edward, Burgoyne decided to send the Germans east to Vermont to steal some.

Lieutenant Colonel Baum, the leader of this raid, neither spoke nor understood English—a serious handicap because, in addition to stealing horses, cattle and wagons, Baum was supposed to enlist any Tories he might find.

Bennington, Vermont, Baum's first objective, was protected by a New Hampshire brigade that had just been raised under the command of the veteran John Stark, who had served at Bunker's Hill, Trenton and Princeton. He was a tall, sinewy, cantankerous man and a born troop leader, who was furious at the Continental Congress because, for political reasons, it had failed to promote him. At the news that Burgoyne's Indians, ranging ahead of Baum, were terrorizing the civilians between the Hudson and Bennington, Stark marched forward to meet the intruders.

Four miles west of Bennington, just inside what is now the New York State line, the two forces came to a halt with the Walloomsac River and a bridge between them. Although Baum did not know it, the Americans outnumbered him by more than two to one, and Colonel Seth Warner's 330 Vermonters were marching south to reinforce Stark.

At about noon, August 16th, two small

American detachments started to swing wide around both German flanks. Stark, with his main strength, stayed in front, waiting for the encirclement to be completed.

The New Hampshire men were using their own muskets, and they had no uniforms. When the flanking parties approached the German rear, they looked like farmers, not soldiers. Baum hoped they were Tories—seeking protection, perhaps, or coming to join the British. Since the German-speaking officer could not question the Americans, he ordered his sentries to let them alone. The New Hampshire men carefully worked themselves into position. Then they opened fire.

In front of Baum's position, Stark gave the order to attack: "There they are! We'll beat them before the night, or Molly Stark will be a widow!"

The Americans rushed the Germans from all sides, driving them together onto a small hill. Baum's men were brave. They stood their ground for two hours, and when their ammunition ran out, they drew their heavy swords, hoping to chop their way out of the American trap. They didn't give up until Baum fell.

Burgoyne, however, had sent reinforcements —a force of Germans under Lieutenant Colonel Breymann that was almost as big as Baum's party. They were a day late in getting to the battlefield. When they did approach Bennington, Stark's men were scattered all over. The New Hampshire recruits had been promised a chance to take anything they wanted from Baum's outfit, and they were combing the German campsite for loot.

Stark was caught off guard. Luckily Warner's reinforcements from Vermont arrived just in time. Breymann, like Baum, mistook the Americans for farmers. Or did, at least, until a squad of New Hampshire men fired at the German column and killed Breymann's horse.

The second battle, on the long, hot afternoon of August 18th, was another American success. The Germans attacked Stark's and Warner's combined forces and found to their dismay that, however unprofessional the Americans appeared, they wouldn't let themselves be outflanked. And on the firing line they gave as good as or better than they got. Breymann was forced to retreat. His drummers beat the signal for a surrender conference. But the Americans, who were more farmers than soldiers, didn't know what the drums were supposed to mean. They kept on shooting, and the German retreat turned into a rout.

When the final score of the two battles at Bennington was added up, the Germans had lost 207 killed and about 700 prisoners. The Americans lost not more than 30 killed and 40 wounded. The Continental Congress, in gratitude, finally appointed Stark a brigadier general in the Continental army.

Burgoyne's plan for the conquest of New York had two prongs. Besides his own main drive down Lake Champlain to the Hudson River, a second, smaller British expedition commanded by Colonel Barry St. Leger was supposed to move on Albany from the northwest. From Oswego, on the shore of Lake Ontario, they were to proceed down the Mohawk River, which joins the Hudson just above Albany.

St. Leger, an experienced officer, had a well-equipped force. One thousand of his men were Indians.

Colonel St. Leger was optimistic. Only one obstacle stood in his path. That was Fort Stanwix, a wilderness post where the city of Rome, New York, now stands. It was held by the 3rd New York Continentals commanded by 28-year-old Peter Gansevoort.

On August 2nd, St. Leger reached Fort Stanwix. He expected Colonel Gansevoort to surrender at the sight of his dazzlingly well-equipped army. The Americans, although outnumbered by more than two to one, had no such intention.

A 50-year-old local landowner, Nicholas Herkimer, a brigadier general in the militia, was marching to Stanwix with 800 volunteers. They might have been a big help to Colonel Gansevoort. But six miles from the fort, at a village called Oriskany, Herkimer's column marched into an Indian ambush arranged by St. Leger. When the savage hand-to-hand struggle was over, Herkimer had lost 200 killed and many more wounded, and he himself had received his death wound. It was lucky that there were any American survivors at all.

No reinforcements got through, but Herkimer's effort helped Gansevoort in another way. For while St. Leger's men were busy at Oriskany, Gansevoort's second in command, Lieutenant Colonel Marinus Willett, led a highly successful raid on the almost-empty British camp. Willett's men made off with twenty-one wagonloads of muskets, ammunition, camp kettles, blankets and clothes. They stripped the Indians' tents of everything they contained, hoping to make the braves think again about the wisdom of aiding King George.

Despite Willett's raid, the British went on preparing to destroy Fort Stanwix, and it looked as if they would do so unless Gansevoort got help.

At Stillwater, just north of Albany, General Schuyler heard about the plight of the Stanwix garrison. Most of Schuyler's officers opposed sending a detachment to rescue Gansevoort; they felt that the American army in front of Albany had more than it could do to hold off Burgoyne.

Schuyler was outraged. He called for a brigadier to command the relief. Benedict Arnold, a major general and Schuyler's second in command, volunteered for a job far below his rank.

Arnold was off, marching as fast as he could with 950 volunteers who were glad to follow him. But he knew when he started for Stanwix that his rescue party was too small to beat St. Leger by force alone. He thought of an ingenious trick.

The Americans held a Tory prisoner sentenced to be hanged for recruiting for the British. This prisoner, named Hon Yost Schuyler, was at least half-insane, and therefore regarded with great respect by the Indians, who thought that madmen were divinely inspired.

Arnold made a bargain with Hon Yost. He promised him a pardon if he would go ahead and tell St. Leger's Indians surrounding Fort Stanwix that a huge party of Americans was about to descend on them.

Hon Yost agreed, and played his part to perfection. The Indians, believing him, mutinied and seized St. Leger's officers' liquor. Two hundred of them, drunk, ran off into the forests. The chiefs of those who remained insisted that St. Leger give the order to retreat. Since the Indians were more than half his force, there was nothing else St. Leger could do.

By the end of August 1777, Burgoyne's plans were not working too well. He had learned that

Howe was not sailing up the Hudson to join him. He had lost 900 men in the Bennington battles. Now he had to face the fact that St. Leger's expedition, the whole western wing of his attack, had collapsed.

Saratoga

To make matters worse for Burgoyne, the strength of the American force that stood between him and Albany had been growing, especially after word spread of the murder of Jane McCrea. It was becoming a pretty good army, too. It included some Continental regiments—Daniel Morgan's riflemen among them—and some first-class militia outfits. Its commander-in-chief was General Horatio Gates, who had replaced General Schuyler on August 19th. Gates, a jolly, 50-year-old former English officer who had lived in Virginia before the war, was an expert on army administration and paperwork. He had both ambition and ability. But on the other hand it had been a long time since he had commanded on a battlefield.

When General Arnold got back from Stanwix, the Americans picked Bemis Heights, overlooking the river road on the west side of the Hudson, as the place to dig in and stand off Burgoyne's attack. Bemis Heights, about ten miles south of the town of Saratoga (now called Schuylerville), had only one serious fault. There was a higher hill slightly west of the bluffs that the Americans had failed to occupy. If Burgoyne could seize it, his gunners would be able to shoot down from above into the American trenches.

The British started from their camp, four miles up the river, on the bright morning of September 19th. They were divided into three sections: one to march down the river road, one to move slightly inland toward Bemis Heights, and the third to sweep around through the woods, trying to surprise the Americans and capture the unoccupied hill.

As the first two British sections approached, the Americans could easily see them coming. Their red coats were brilliant. Their polished steel bayonets glistened in the sunlight. For three hours, while the British attack shaped up, Gates did nothing at all. Arnold, his second in command, begged to be allowed to advance to meet Burgoyne's assault. But Gates seemed to think that the Americans were safe inside their crude fortifications. Finally he woke up. He realized that there might be some threat to the American left flank, and he ordered Morgan's riflemen and Henry Dearborn's light infantry to guard against it. If they ran into trouble, they could call on Arnold's other men for help.

Morgan's sharpshooters attacked Burgoyne's flanking division near a place called Freeman's

Farm, and a furious fight developed. Arnold's men hurried to help. The battle raged across a clearing in the woods of some twenty acres. The Americans had the best of the shooting, but every time they drove the British from the field, Burgoyne's men returned by charging with their bayonets. Arnold, who was directing the battle, felt sure that with more American troops he could break the British line. Gates, still sitting in the fortifications, refused to give him the men. Arnold's golden opportunity was lost. Help came for the badly mauled British from their third division down on the river road, and the Americans retreated to their fortifications. The Americans had won a victory—their casualties were only half as many as Burgoyne's—but not a decisive one. The British camped on the battlefield.

That ended the first half of the Battle of Saratoga—so called because Saratoga was where, finally, the surrender took place.

More than two weeks passed before Burgoyne struck again. He waited because he hoped that General Henry Clinton, far to the south, might be able to help him. Clinton, who had been left behind in New York City when Howe went to Philadelphia, attacked and captured two American forts on the west bank of the Hudson at Bear Mountain—Forts Clinton and Montgomery. But, having done so, he went back to New York City. Burgoyne waited in vain.

On the American side, in the meantime, Gates and Arnold had a falling out. Gates, in writing his report to Congress, did not even mention the name of Arnold, the man who had won the battle for him. The two generals had a bitter quarrel. Gates relieved Arnold of his command and excluded him from headquarters. Arnold, an officer without a job, stayed in the Bemis Heights camp.

By October 7th, Burgoyne felt he could no longer wait to hear from Clinton. He had to capture Albany before winter. Since he wasn't quite sure what to do, Burgoyne planned a strong reconnaissance by more than 1,500 of the British troops to see if the Americans had occupied the high hill west of Bemis Heights. They had.

Burgoyne's reconnaissance had barely started before the American outpost guards spotted it. This time Gates reacted quickly. Morgan's riflemen and General Enoch Poor's brigade promptly threw themselves against the British column. Dearborn's light infantry was right on Morgan's heels. Both ends of the British line were beaten back, and Burgoyne sent his aide to order a general retreat. Before the aide could deliver the command, he was shot and captured.

At this moment Benedict Arnold, riding a huge brown horse, galloped onto the field. He had no command, but he simply could not bear to stay in camp, doing nothing, with a fight in progress.

The first soldiers Arnold met—part of Poor's brigade—were militiamen from Norwich, Connecticut, his hometown. They gave him a rousing cheer. Arnold raced on, overtook the head of General Ebenezer Learned's brigade, and led three of its regiments in a charge against German troops in the center of the British line.

But the British troops were led by General Simon Fraser, as brave and inspiring a field officer as Arnold himself. Fraser dashed up and down the line, rallying the British troops. It was not until Fraser fell, picked off by one of Morgan's marksmen, that the British gave up. The entire line gave way and fell back to their entrenchments immediately north of Freeman's Farm.

That seemed to be the end of the battle.

But Arnold was not done. He was not satisfied with winning the field. He wanted a smashing victory.

Arnold led one party in a furious charge against a section of the British fortifications. Then he rode straight across the line of fire and organized another attack on a fortification full of German soldiers led by Lieutenant Colonel Breymann, who had been beaten at Bennington. Arnold galloped around to the back of the strong point, and into it. His brown horse was shot. Arnold was hit in the leg with a bullet that broke his thigh bone—the same leg that had been wounded at Quebec. He had to be carried off the field—victorious, but lamed for life.

A week later at Saratoga, Burgoyne, having thought over his losses, surrendered. It was a tremendous American victory. When Burgoyne handed Gates his sword, King George's fighting forces lost seven British generals, 300 other officers and more than 5,000 enlisted men—along with 5,000 muskets, 27 cannons and stores of all kinds of equipment.

❧ 13
Valley Forge
and the Conway Cabal

After Saratoga, Gates sat down and wrote a report of his victory. Instead of addressing the letter to Washington, his commander-in-chief, Gates reported directly to the Continental Congress at York, Pennsylvania. It was no accident. For Gates, basking in the praise he was getting, was beginning to think he was a candidate for Washington's job.

Gates ordered his aide, Colonel James Wilkinson, to deliver the report. On his trip south, Wilkinson did everything he could to make fun of Washington and to praise his boss, Gates—whose sudden popularity was mainly due to Arnold's battlefield leadership. Among other things, Wilkinson said he had read a letter written to Gates by Brigadier General Thomas Conway, a French officer who had signed a contract to come over and fight for the Americans. Conway felt he deserved to be at least an American major general, and that Washington's military talents were "miserable." Gates and Conway, both jealous of

Washington, made a pair of natural allies. Wilkinson, riding toward York, quoted Conway's letter to everybody who would listen. He didn't fail to include Conway's sarcastic comment that God must have made up his mind to save America, for otherwise, under as weak a general as Washington, she would have already lost the war.

When Wilkinson finally reached York, the Congress—with most of the delegates away—promoted him to brigadier general, a slap in the face to countless American officers who had done more than slander General Washington to earn promotion. To make matters worse, Congress reorganized the Board of War—a powerful committee—and elected Gates its president. Then Congress made Conway a major general and the army's inspector general.

If anything less than the fate of his country had been involved, Washington would have resigned.

But Washington, above almost all Americans, believed that Congress should be superior to the military power. And he wasn't positive that Congress, by promoting his critics, intended to insult him. Washington stayed on.

The intrigue against Washington was called the "Conway Cabal." (Cabal means conspiracy.) Besides Gates and Conway, its leaders were Richard Henry Lee and Francis Lee of Virginia, Benjamin Rush and Thomas Mifflin of Pennsylvania, and Sam Adams and James Lovell of Massachusetts.

All of these men undoubtedly wanted to put Gates in Washington's place as commander-in-chief, but perhaps not all of them were really conspirators. Rush and Lovell, for instance, were seriously afraid that Washington, beloved and trusted by soldiers and civilians alike, had ambitions to become an American king.

The cold winter of 1777–78, which Washington and the Continental Army spent at Valley Forge, became a legend—an incredible tale not only of physical suffering but of moral heroism. The troops lacked food, clothing and decent shelter. The country's neglect of its fighting men was all the more horrible because much of it was unnecessary. There needn't have been any starvation, for instance. There was food within reach —if the farmers had been willing to accept Continental paper money in payment for it.

Despite the discouraging maneuvers against him in Congress, and despite the hardships of Valley Forge, Washington stayed with his army. His men, in return, remained loyal to him. Although many of his soldiers left when their enlistments expired, and others deserted, many stayed. Those who did remain became the backbone of a new Continental Army.

Toward spring, things took a turn for the better. Another European volunteer had joined the Americans—Baron Friedrich von Steuben, a stocky, robust former German army captain.

Valley Forge, Pennsylvania. In huts like this reconstructed
one, George Washington's army suffered through the cold
winter of 1777–1778.

Steuben, with Washington's blessing, began to teach the wretched men at Valley Forge the elementary military skills that even those who had served for two or three years had never had a chance to learn. He did a wonderful job. He worked twelve hours a day, every day, driving the men hard and giving Washington's soldiers their first basic training.

The situation at York was also improving. When the absent delegates returned to Congress from their home states and saw what Washington's political enemies had done while they were away, Congress dropped Gates from the Board of War. And in Conway's place as inspector general, it put Baron von Steuben. Even the supply situation improved. Nathanael Greene, one of Washington's best generals, was given the thankless job of quartermaster. And he managed to find the army some food, some shoes and some decent clothing.

By the end of spring 1778, America once more had a fighting force. Despite the horrors of winter camp, despite the men's suffering, it was a better army than it had ever been before.

❧ 14
The Battle of Monmouth

While the Americans had been freezing and starving at Valley Forge, the British enjoyed a snug winter in Philadelphia. In May 1778, General Howe, who had asked to be relieved because he no longer saw any chance of ending the rebellion, went home to England. His place as British commander-in-chief was taken by Sir Henry Clinton, a fussy but competent officer. Clinton's first job, on orders from London, was to retreat from Philadelphia to New York City.

The British, 10,000 strong, began to leave on June 16, 1778. At first the Americans were confused about Clinton's plans, but as soon as Washington understood what the British were doing, he wanted to attack. There were 12,000 well-drilled men in the American army. Washington hoped he could head off the British columns and inflict real damage on the enemy.

Unfortunately, the boastful General Charles Lee, who had been traded for a British general in an exchange of prisoners, had returned to duty.

Neither Washington nor Congress knew that by this time Lee believed that Americans couldn't fight and were bound to lose the war. While he was a prisoner Lee had written out a plan for their defeat, which he had given to Howe.

As the Americans' senior major general, Lee was entitled to lead the attack on the British. The plan was to have Lee, with the forward section of Washington's army, catch up with Clinton's column and lure as many British as possible into a fight. Then Washington, with the main strength of the American army, would come forward to deliver the crushing blow.

On the hot morning of June 28th, Lee caught up with the British near Monmouth Courthouse, New Jersey. This was not very far south of Sandy Hook, which meant safety for Clinton, for from there his army could travel to New York by ship. Lee advanced halfheartedly, and the British turned on Lee's troops, formed a battle line and got set to meet an attack.

Instead of holding his ground and calling on Washington for reinforcements, Lee ordered a retreat. In the sweltering heat—the temperature reached 96 degrees in the shade—Lee's 5,000 men trudged back the way they had come. To make his fantastic blunder complete, Lee failed to tell Washington what he had done.

Washington, confident that Lee was doing well, was marching forward with the main body of troops. As he approached the battlefield, he saw American soldiers walking the wrong way. They told him Lee had ordered a retreat. Washington couldn't believe it. He even ordered one soldier arrested for spreading false rumors.

Finally Washington had to face the shocking truth, because he met Lee himself. In a fury Washington ordered Lee, in disgrace, to the rear. Then the commander-in-chief turned the troops around and, with Greene, Lafayette and Wayne, organized the Americans into a line to stop the British pursuit.

Now the British had the advantage that Lee had lost. But the Americans proved how much they had learned under Steuben's firm hand. The fighting was furious. Four times the British hurled themselves against the Americans, and four times the Americans beat back the assaults.

The battle of Monmouth produced the best-known lady gunner in American history—Molly Pitcher, whose real name was Mary Hays. Her husband, who had once been an artilleryman, fought with the Americans at Monmouth as an infantryman. Molly started the day carrying pitchers of water to men who were wounded. Then her husband, noticing that a gunner had been shot, put down his musket to help fire the cannon. He, in turn, was wounded. Molly took his place and kept the cannon firing until Washington's reinforcements arrived.

Washington was by no means satisfied with merely standing off four attacks. He wanted a real victory. He organized an American counterattack, but darkness fell before he could get it under way.

The chance was gone. The British rested a few hours and, around midnight, slipped away toward Sandy Hook. By July 5th, to Washington's intense disappointment, Clinton's army was safe in New York City.

Monmouth was the last big Revolutionary War battle in the North, because the British changed their grand strategy. They decided to hold New York City but to attack in the South, conquer the Carolinas and then move into Virginia.

The northern campaigns had certainly been discouraging to the British, who had been so confident in 1775. Not only had they lost battles but they had lost a political struggle as well. France no longer thought that King George could smash the American rebellion, and in February 1778, she had signed a treaty with the Continental Congress.

France had been secretly helping the Americans since 1776. At that time Congress had sent Silas Deane (a Connecticut merchant) and Benjamin Franklin (Pennsylvania's elder statesman) to Paris to try to persuade France to make her secret assistance open and official—to become America's ally.

France had hesitated, wondering whether the

Americans really had a chance, until after the brilliant American success at Saratoga. That's why the Saratoga campaign, very properly, is called the turning point of the Revolutionary War.

By July 1778, France and Great Britain were officially at war. A great advantage of the French alliance, from the American point of view, was the cooperation of the first-class French navy. America had started building a navy of her own—an expensive, slow process. The American fleet was small. It was capable of brave, dashing feats, but by itself it was no match for the British navy's vast array of powerful men-of-war.

The first attempt at a combined operation with the French fleet—an effort to capture Newport, Rhode Island, from the British—was a dismal failure. For a long time afterward the French and Americans distrusted each other. It took great tact on the part of Rochambeau, the French general, and Washington and Lafayette to make the new alliance work.

Among other things, France and America had different ideas about the proper scope of the war. The French were interested in attacking the British West Indies. The Americans, on the other hand, wanted France to concentrate on the fighting in the thirteen colonies.

Nevertheless, anything that caused trouble for Great Britain was at least an indirect help to the Americans. In 1779, for instance, Spain joined the global war against England. The Spanish King disapproved of revolutions against Kings, so that Spain did not become an ally of America. Spain was simply trying to chip a few pieces off the far-flung British Empire. Whatever Spain's motives, Americans were glad to have another nation added to the list of their own enemy's enemies.

❧ 15
The British Conquer in the South

In the South, especially in the Carolinas, Clinton hoped to find a great many American Tories ready to rally to the King's support. There were, in fact, a good many Americans in the South—just as there were in the North—who were not in favor of the American rebellion and whose loyalties were still with England. But there were not nearly so many as the British imagined.

In November 1779, the British fleet sailed for Savannah, Georgia, convoying some 3,000 of Clinton's men in transports. This was the first British activity in the South since June 1776, when they had failed in a seaborne attempt to take Charleston, South Carolina. Things went much better for them this time. There were only 800 Americans to oppose them. Savannah fell easily into British hands, and the Americans retreated into South Carolina. That let all Georgia go to the British by default.

A year later, in September, the Americans and the French tried to dislodge the British from

Savannah, but this combined operation, like the attack on Newport, was an expensive failure.

Clinton, in New York, was encouraged by the British successes at Savannah to try a similar, larger operation against Charleston. With his second in command, General Charles Cornwallis, Clinton sailed south with an 8,500-man army. The British landed near Charleston in February 1780, and spent the next two months building up their strength to a most impressive 10,000.

That was twice the size of the American force in Charleston, which was made up of Continentals and militiamen in about equal number and was commanded by General Benjamin Lincoln of Massachusetts.

The contest was decided before the fighting began. The Americans hadn't a chance. They couldn't retreat because the British surrounded them. General Lincoln surrendered Charleston on May 12th, losing not only the city but his complete army with all its weapons, equipment and precious stocks of ammunition.

The British promptly fanned out from Charleston into the interior of the state. No one opposed them because Lincoln had surrendered all the soldiers available to defend South Carolina. Clinton established British bases at Camden, at Cheraw and at Fort 96 near Greenwood. Then, thinking everything was under control, he headed back to New York City, leaving Cornwallis to

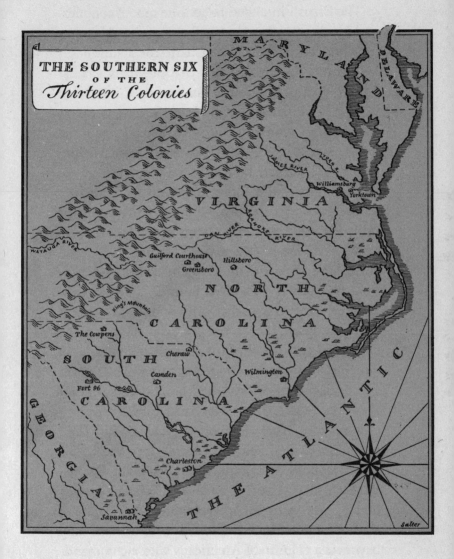

THE SOUTHERN SIX
OF THE
Thirteen Colonies

MARYLAND

DELAWARE

JAMES RIVER

YORK R.

Williamsburg

Yorktown

VIRGINIA

DAN RIVER

ROANOKE RIVER

WATAUGA RIVER

Guilford Courthouse

Hillsboro

Greensboro

NORTH

King's Mountain

CAROLINA

The Cowpens

SOUTH

Cheraw

Camden

Wilmington

Fort 96

CAROLINA

GEORGIA

Charleston

THE ATLANTIC

Savannah

Salter

advance from South Carolina into North Carolina.

The British intended to act like model conquerors in the South. Cornwallis had let Lincoln's militiamen go home after Charleston's surrender, on their oaths never again to bear arms against King George. And in the same spirit Clinton had used detachments of American Tories, as far as possible, to man his South Carolina bases. The result was a bitter, ferocious civil war swirling around each of the British strong points.

The sight of the Tories organized to fight their fellow countrymen was more than the unarmed militia, returning to their farms and villages, could bear. They broke their word, rearmed, formed small raiding parties under such famous leaders as Francis Marion, Thomas Sumter and Andrew Pickens. For more than three months, South Carolina was the scene of countless savage engagements—most of them small and short—in which the rules of war were forgotten. The British and Tories hanged the American raiders whenever they could catch them. The Americans, answering cruelty with cruelty, found it easier to kill their enemies than to take prisoners. It was in this bitter, confused struggle that Lieutenant Colonel Banastre Tarleton, a brilliant British cavalry officer, won most of his reputation for frightful cruelty. His men slaughtered with swords and bayonets a column of Americans whose commander had not only raised a white surrender flag but

114

had ordered his men to lay down their weapons.

Peace for South Carolina, British style, turned out to be a model all the other states hoped to avoid.

General Washington had sent Maryland and Delaware Continentals, under Major General Baron de Kalb, south to help General Lincoln. But de Kalb, a giant of a man and an extremely capable French officer, had only reached North Carolina's northern border when Charleston surrendered.

Congress hesitated about giving command of the entire southern army to a foreigner. Without asking Washington's advice, it picked General Gates as Lincoln's replacement. Gates was delighted. He had been timid at Saratoga; now he was ready to make up for the hesitation he had shown. Gates caught up with de Kalb in North Carolina on July 25th, took over the small column of Delawares and Marylanders, and ordered an immediate march straight for Camden, South Carolina. Gates's officers and men, on hearing this order, looked at each other with blank amazement. The route he picked was an impossible road through swamps and deep sand in Tory country. The inhabitants of this section were so short of food themselves that the soldiers were certain to go hungry. Gates refused to listen to his officers' plea to take another, better road.

Two weeks later when the Americans, in the

last stages of exhaustion, reached Camden, they found a British force twice their size waiting for them. The Americans blundered into contact with Cornwallis' troops. De Kalb was in favor of withdrawing while there was still time. Gates overruled him.

The battlefield, north of Camden, was a thin forest of pines with swamps on both its sides. The Americans and British formed battle lines very early on the morning of August 16, 1780. The British advanced.

At the first British bayonet charge, Gates's militiamen—half the American force—ran off in panic. To his undying shame, Gates, whose horse was the fastest in the American army, ran with them. That left de Kalb with the American Continentals, now hopelessly outnumbered, to carry on the fight. And fight they did, with the utmost bravery, until de Kalb, slashed on the head by a saber stroke and hit with eleven bullets, collapsed, fatally wounded. "Bloody" Tarleton's cavalrymen swept through the pines, and the Americans—some of the best fighters in the army—scattered in complete disorder, trying to find hiding places in the swamps.

Gates, who had insisted on the insane march and the hopeless battle, ran on and on, all the way to Hillsboro, North Carolina—200 miles in three and a half days. "Was there ever an instance of a general running away, as Gates has done, from his whole army?" asked Alexander Hamilton. America laughed at Gates, but the joke was not very funny. Lincoln had lost one army. Gates had lost another. It was not going to be easy to find a third.

Congress recalled Gates. This time Congress had the good sense to ask Washington to appoint the new commander for the Southern Department.

There was no question in Washington's mind about the best man for the job. He immediately chose General Nathanael Greene.

🎜 16
America's Most Famous Traitor

The year 1780, in which Gates's reputation was ruined, was also the year in which Benedict Arnold, Gates's old rival, was exposed as a traitor.

It was a sad story which began when Washington, looking for a post that his dashing field officer could manage in spite of his wounded leg, made Arnold military governor of Philadelphia. In no time at all, Arnold and Pennsylvania's civilian authorities were at each other's throats. Arnold was arrogant, unwilling to try to compromise with the civilian point of view. The Philadelphians were suspicious of military men, and they thought Arnold was too lenient with Tories and war profiteers. They disapproved of his courting Peggy Shippen, a girl twenty years his junior who had danced with British officers in Philadelphia during the winter Washington's army had spent at Valley Forge.

By 1779 Arnold and the Pennsylvania government were practically at war. Pennsylvania complained to the Continental Congress, and Congress ordered Arnold to face a court-martial.

While awaiting trial, confident that he would be cleared, Arnold married Miss Shippen.

Then came the first step toward treason.

Mrs. Arnold knew a handsome young British officer, Major John André, who had been stationed in Philadelphia and was now on Clinton's staff in New York City. The Arnolds wrote secretly to André, offering to desert the American cause and fight for the British.

André answered the Arnolds' letter, but nothing was settled. Then came the trial. In January 1780, the military court found that, while Arnold had not committed any crimes, he had been imprudent. It ordered Washington to give him an official reprimand.

Arnold was furious. The truth was that he had been involved in several shady, unimportant—and unsuccessful—deals. Washington, who respected the man's great fighting ability, made the reprimand as mild as possible. But because he had not been completely cleared, Arnold was ready to close his bargain with the British.

He agreed to do more than change sides. Arnold promised to betray the fort at West Point and at least 3,000 American soldiers for £20,000 and a high command in the British army.

Then he asked Washington, who had done his

best to keep from hurting Arnold's feelings, to give him the command at West Point. Washington did so.

There remained one last step—a face-to-face conference between Arnold and some British army representative to settle the details of the betrayal. Ambitious Major André, who had been working on the plot for more than a year, insisted on going to meet Arnold himself. A British warship, the *Vulture,* took André up the Hudson, and he was rowed ashore in the dark by two tenants on the estate of Joshua Smith, near Haverstraw. There André and Arnold sat on the riverbank, talking from midnight to dawn. At daybreak they moved to Smith's house because it seemed too dangerous to row André back to the *Vulture* when he might be seen.

Arnold gave André the plans of West Point and some other secret papers. Then he returned to his West Point headquarters while André hid for the day in Smith's attic.

American shore batteries fired on the *Vulture,* and Smith decided that even at night it would be too dangerous to row André back to his ship. He thought André should return to New York City by land, and he offered to guide André through the American lines if André would take off his British uniform and disguise himself in civilian clothes. It was a dreadful risk for André to take, for that made him a spy. If captured, he would surely be hanged.

André called himself "John Anderson" and carried a pass in that name, signed by Arnold. The secret papers were hidden in his stocking. He got safely past the southernmost American post when three young men stopped him. They meant to rob him. They made André take off his clothes to make sure he wasn't hiding any money, and they found the papers in his stocking.

Whatever else they may have been, the three young men were patriots. When they saw the plans of West Point, they escorted André back to the American army post at North Castle.

Lieutenant Colonel Jameson, who commanded there, was suspicious. He noticed that the secret papers were in the same handwriting as the pass—Benedict Arnold's. Instead of sending both the documents and the strange prisoner back to West Point, as his standing orders demanded, Jameson forwarded the papers to General Washington. To protect himself—and before sending André, under guard, to Arnold—he sent Arnold a note telling what had happened and what he had done.

By coincidence Washington was on his way to inspect West Point. As soon as the note from Jameson arrived, Arnold realized that the game was up. He bolted out of his house, raced down to the Hudson and escaped to the *Vulture*.

Washington arrived at Arnold's house later that same day, September 25th. He waited for Arnold. The messenger with the secret papers had missed him on the road, and Washington suspected nothing until the afternoon, when the rider carrying the telltale evidence against Arnold finally delivered it.

Arnold reached New York City and the safety of the British camp. André was tried by court-martial and hanged as a spy. He died bravely, and all over America those who felt sorry for him—and there were many who did—told stories of his charm and courage.

André's death was tragic. So had been the death of an American spy, Nathan Hale, who was hanged by the British in 1776 just after the capture of New York City. Hale was caught behind the British lines, dressed as a civilian. He was arrested one day and hanged the next. This is not to say that one death canceled out another, or that André was hanged because Hale had been hanged. But only that, in war, the fate of spies who are caught is tragically certain.

〆 17
King's Mountain and Cowpens

Before a third American army had time to take the field in the South, a determined body of southern frontiersmen handed the British a surprising defeat.

Cornwallis, after his victory at Camden, looked forward to the conquest of all of North Carolina, and he called for the aid of Major Patrick Ferguson, who was at Fort 96. Ferguson was a scrappy commander who had organized several thousand South Carolina Tories into British units. With them he had terrorized the whole district, raiding, looting and hanging "rebels." No one hated Ferguson and his Tories more than the sharp-shooting frontiersmen who lived along the Watauga River on the west side of the Blue Ridge Mountains in what is now Tennessee.

Ferguson thought he'd give the Watauga men a good licking before he joined Cornwallis.

He sent word that he was going to cross the mountains and put a stop to the frontiersmen's foolish resistance to British peace. The Watauga men, thinking it over, decided that they'd rather attack Ferguson on *his* side of the mountains and avoid having their farms and cabins burned. They got together at the end of September 1780. Volunteers from all along the frontier joined them, and they started out to track down the despised Tory raiders.

The frontiersmen moved fast. Most of them rode horses, although they planned to fight as infantrymen, not cavalry. The weather was cold and rainy. The party was short of food, and the ground on which they slept was wet. But these were rugged men, many of them experienced Indian fighters to whom physical hardships were an everyday matter.

They caught Ferguson on October 7th. They outnumbered the Tories about 1,400 to 1,100. But Ferguson had had time to take an extremely strong defensive position on the flat top of King's Mountain on the North Carolina–South Carolina border, near Gastonia, North Carolina. The sides of the mountain were steep and rocky.

The frontiersmen surrounded the base of the mountain. Indian war whoops were their signal to attack. Up the mountainside they scrambled, shooting as they climbed.

Ferguson's Tories charged with bayonets, a weapon the frontiersmen didn't have. On the other hand, the Americans were sharpshooters. They climbed into the trees with their long-barreled rifles, took careful aim and picked off Ferguson's men one by one. The deadly, accurate fire won out. The frontiersmen swarmed onto the level mountaintop. The fighting raged on, but only because Ferguson, who had sworn he'd never surrender to the "bandits," drove his Tories far past the point where most of them were ready to give up. Finally a sharpshooter's bullet stopped Ferguson. He fell from his horse and died.

Now it was the frontiersmen who wouldn't stop. Their fury—after the months in which Ferguson's Tories had been the terror of the countryside—was so great that they wanted to kill every Tory. But in the end they listened to their officers' pleas and took some 700 prisoners. As a fighting unit, Ferguson's Tories no longer existed.

Cornwallis, at Charlotte, North Carolina, was scared when he heard the news from King's Mountain. He imagined an uprising in South Carolina that might destroy his bases one at a time and demolish the foundations of his North Carolina plans. He pulled back from Charlotte to Winnsboro, South Carolina.

But Cornwallis' fears were premature. The Watauga men, having done what they had set out to do, went home. There was no real danger to the British, and no real American army in the South until after Greene arrived at Hillsboro and took over from Gates on December 2nd. Even then, the "Grand Army" of the South, including about 700 survivors of Camden, was a pitifully small force. The Continental Congress was nearly bankrupt. All the way south, Greene had literally begged for men, muskets, supplies—even hay for his horses. His total strength came to 1,500 infantrymen fit for duty, 90 cavalrymen and 60 artillerymen. And only half of them were fully equipped.

Greene's army was no match for even a small part of Cornwallis' army, and it was just lucky that Cornwallis didn't guess the truth.

At this miserable moment, Greene made a masterful move. He would need time to retrain, refit and reinforce. Hillsboro, which had seen more than it wanted of the American army, was no place to do so. Greene, defying all the rules of military science, split his small army into two divisions. He sent one of them, commanded by Daniel Morgan, to the west. He took the other south to Cheraw, South Carolina.

The strategy was brilliant, and the risk was great. It looked as if Greene were almost asking Cornwallis to gobble up his two tiny divisions. But, for one thing, Greene knew that he had a much better chance of getting food for his men by dividing them into two groups. In the second place, he hoped to confuse Cornwallis. If the British chased Morgan, Greene could march straight to Charleston. If they chased Greene, Morgan could strike at Fort 96 and Augusta.

Six weeks later Cornwallis reacted. He ordered Tarleton, with 1,100 men, cavalry, infantry and a few artillerymen, to chase Morgan. Tarleton didn't have to chase him far, for Morgan, with reinforcements, had close to 1,000 men in his division, and he was ready to stand and fight. Morgan picked Cowpens, just north of Spartanburg, South Carolina, as the battlefield. It was a wide plain dotted with tall trees, and got its name from its use as a place to round up range cattle. On the evening of January 16, 1781, "Old Wagoner" Morgan wandered through the camp, chatting and joking with his men around their campfires. He told them to settle down and get a good night's sleep.

The next morning Morgan arranged his battle lines. His plan was unusual and wise. It was based on what his inexperienced troops could do best— shoot—and not on complicated maneuvers. He did not expect the impossible.

Morgan scattered 150 of his best marksmen in the front line and behind them placed two ranks of Carolina militiamen, his weakest troops. Behind them, on slightly higher ground, he put his strongest units—Maryland and Delaware Continentals and Virginia volunteers who had served in the Continental Army. At the rear, behind the low hill, he posted 80 horsemen commanded by Lieutenant Colonel William Washington, who was a distant cousin of the general. These horsemen and 45 Georgia cavalrymen were Morgan's reserves.

Morgan told every man in his outfit exactly what he wanted. The sharpshooters were to hide behind trees and wait till the enemy got to within 150 feet. Then they were to take careful aim and make every shot count. After only two volleys the sharpshooters could fall back to the second line— the militia—firing as they withdrew. The militia were asked to aim carefully and to stay as long as they could. But when they felt they had had all the punishment they could stand, they were to retreat. They were to march around behind the Continentals. There they would form up to fight again if they wished.

After he had explained everything, Morgan told the men to "ease their joints"—to sit down in their battle formations and save their energies.

Tarleton had been pushing his men toward Morgan since long before dawn. He reached Cowpens around eight o'clock on the morning of January 17th and led a small party of cavalry up front to look over the situation. Tarleton spotted the front-line sharpshooters and immediately told his horsemen to ride them down. The sharpshooters, as ordered, waited till the horsemen were very close, aimed carefully and trooper after trooper fell out of his saddle.

Nonetheless Tarleton ordered his main attack.

128

The British headed for the second American line, which the sharpshooters had now joined. The Carolina militiamen fired carefully, with devastating effect. In spite of terrible losses, the British pushed ahead.

Now the militia started to retreat according to plan. Tarleton, thinking the Americans were defeated, ordered his cavalry to pursue them. But William Washington's horsemen suddenly galloped up from the rear, beat Tarleton's men back and covered the militia's withdrawal.

Even so, the British were convinced the battle was practically won. Shouting, they charged Morgan's third line. The Continentals did not give way.

Then the Americans made a mistake. Tarleton ordered some of his men to attack one of the American flanks. Lieutenant Colonel John E. Howard, who commanded the Continentals, saw the British flanking move and ordered some of his men to face sideways to meet it. Somehow his order was misunderstood. The whole Continental line, thinking a withdrawal had been ordered, started to pull back.

Morgan rode up and asked Howard what was happening. Howard explained the accident. Morgan calmly said, "We'll find another position for you."

Once again Tarleton was sure the Americans had been beaten. He told his whole line to fall on them. The British broke ranks and charged forward.

William Washington, on horseback, could see that the British had broken their formations. He sent a messenger to Morgan with word that the British were "coming on like a mob." "One good fire" from the infantry, Washington said, was all he needed. Then he'd charge in with his cavalry and finish the British off.

"Face about!" Morgan shouted to the Continentals. "Give them one good fire, and the day is ours."

By this time the British had come over the hill where the Continentals had first stood, and were rushing down the rear slopes. They were only 150 feet from the Americans when the whole line of Continentals turned and blazed away. Their fire stopped the British. Now the Continentals lowered their bayonets and charged. There was stubborn fighting—and the Americans won. Tarleton himself got away from William Washington, but he had lost nine-tenths of his troops and a large part of his terrifying reputation.

❧ 18
What Nathanael Greene Did

Right after Cowpens, Morgan marched north. When Greene, at Cheraw, heard of the victory a week later, he got on his horse and streaked cross-country to join Morgan.

Now Morgan and Greene both knew that, while Morgan had been able to beat Tarleton's detachment, the Americans were far from ready to engage Cornwallis' main army. Cornwallis was chasing Morgan, but Morgan moved fast. After five days Cornwallis realized his army was going to have to pick up speed. He ordered his units to strip down to what the soldiers themselves could carry. They even had to burn their tents. The British, for once, were almost as badly supplied as the Americans.

When Greene heard about it, he was overjoyed. "Then he is ours!" he exclaimed.

Greene's remark may seem odd, since his small army was still pursued by a big army he didn't dare fight. But Greene knew from his own experience that there was practically no food and shelter in North Carolina. He knew how hard it was going to be to march across the sandy pine plains and through the swamps and rivers swollen by February rains. And his bold plan was to keep Cornwallis running after him, leading the British into exhaustion all the way to the Virginia border. Brave and well-trained though they were, Cornwallis' men were used to a well-managed army that fed them on time and kept them warm and dry. Greene was sure that the British would suffer much more under wretched conditions than his own men.

Greene headed for the Dan River on Virginia's southern border. The idea of the race to the Dan was so daring that even Morgan was scared. The Americans had to keep ahead of the British, but never so far ahead that the British would call a halt to the chase. Greene was a great organizer. When he sent officers ahead to see that there were boats waiting for his army at every river, those boats were there. Sometimes the Americans crossed less than a rifle shot ahead of the British—but they always got across.

Greene won the race. As he had calculated, Cornwallis dared not follow him into Virginia. For the time being, the only army in North Carolina was British. But the rigors of the chase showed. Many of the British soldiers were sick. All were exhausted. The rate of desertions increased sharply. When Cornwallis marched back to Hillsboro proclaiming the final defeat of the rebellion in North Carolina, nobody—not even the most optimistic North Carolina Tories—believed him.

Indeed, by March, Greene's army which had rested and added reinforcements felt strong enough to reenter North Carolina. This time Greene was hunting for Cornwallis.

The Americans by now were 4,000 strong, perhaps twice the number in Cornwallis' army. The catch was that only 630 of Greene's men were trained Continentals. Morgan had gone home after the race to the Dan because the damp weather had given him arthritis. But when Greene found Cornwallis, he borrowed Morgan's excellent way of keeping the militia from panicking.

The battle was fought at Guilford Courthouse, north of Greensboro, North Carolina, on March 15, 1781. Like Morgan at Cowpens, Greene asked the militia to stand long enough to fire only twice, and then to retire in good order. They obeyed.

When Cornwallis' men rammed into the Continentals, the Americans would not budge. Neither would the British. The field became a terrible mass of musket clubbing, bayonet stabbing and deadly hand-to-hand fights. Cornwallis felt he had to win at any cost. Seeing that Greene's Continentals could not be beaten back, he ordered his artillery to fire into the confusion of the struggling front line. The guns killed about as many British as Americans. It was a desperate last resort.

Greene did not realize how close Cornwallis was to defeat. He did know that he could not lose his army. In the face of the murderous artillery barrage, Greene decided to retire.

Cornwallis held the field, but he had lost about a quarter of his men and a large proportion of his officers. His victory was worthless. He could not feed his army in the neighborhood, and had to march his worn-out men 200 miles to the nearest British supply depot at Wilmington. This was the only town in all of North Carolina that the British still controlled.

Greene, who in four amazing months had reduced Cornwallis' army from a powerful striking force into a mere ghost of its former self, headed for South Carolina. He hoped to rout the British out of their interior posts—like Fort 96 and Camden—and drive them back, along with their Tory volunteers, to the seacoast. Greene did exactly that. With his ragged, hungry men, sometimes helped by local militia, Greene fought a series of small battles. He couldn't afford big risks, so he never won decisive victories. Occasionally he lost an engagement. Yet every time the British "won" a battle from Greene and counted their dead, they decided to retreat.

By the fall of 1781, the British had withdrawn to Charleston and Savannah. The rest of the South belonged to the Americans. And Greene's military reputation was second only to Washington's. The commander-in-chief had long regarded Greene as his ablest general. Now the whole country understood why.

~~ 19
Yorktown

When Greene turned south, Cornwallis headed north. He marched from Wilmington to Virginia in April 1781, and joined a large British detachment whose most active commander was Benedict Arnold, the traitor.

Arnold had changed sides, but he was still a dangerous fighting man. For five months his force had been raiding, burning and laying waste to the Virginia countryside. The wide, slow-moving Virginia rivers were lined with storehouses full of food and tobacco. Cornwallis, with Arnold, burned them, along with whatever military supply depots they could find.

All this time George Washington and the main Continental army had been holding Clinton's 15,000-man army in check—hoping, year after year, to strike at the British in New York City. Washington's hopes had sometimes seemed much too optimistic. His hands had been full just trying to keep the American army from falling apart. He had been plagued by mutinies and desertions. His recruiting campaigns had failed.

In June 1781, Washington's army contained no more than 5,000 men—in contrast to the 37,000 Congress had asked the states to provide. His great interest was still New York City, where most of the British were stationed.

At the same time, Washington could scarcely ignore the looting of Virginia. Besides, he wanted to capture Benedict Arnold and bring the traitor to justice. Washington gave Lafayette 1,200 men and sent him down to Virginia.

As it happened, Arnold was recalled north soon after Lafayette took the field. Cornwallis, with about 5,500 men, continued the Arnold-style war of raiding and burning. (Arnold escaped the Americans, went to England after the war and lived wretchedly for twenty more years.)

Bit by bit the Americans built up a force in Virginia. Wayne and Steuben joined Lafayette. But even so, Cornwallis' men scored one hit-and-run success after another. It occurred to Cornwallis that the British could use a permanent Virginia shore base—a place where supplies and reinforcements from New York could be landed and stored. He chose a small port, Yorktown, where the York River flows into the Chesapeake Bay. He moved his army there in June and started to fortify the base.

In the meantime, Washington had learned that a huge French fleet was coming to America, bringing more French soldiers with it. His hopes of recapturing New York City rose. Washington conferred with General Rochambeau, commander of the 4,500-man French army in America, and they worked out plans for a French-American attack on Clinton's New York City stronghold.

But it turned out that the French fleet could stay in American waters only until October, and it didn't even sail from the West Indies until the middle of August. That would scarcely leave time enough for as tough an operation as the planned assault on New York City.

Washington decided to use the French fleet where he could—Virginia. He left a few troops outside New York, keeping up a pretense that his army was still there, and headed south late in August. The French, under Rochambeau, marched with him.

In September the British dispatched part of their navy to the Chesapeake Bay area, but France's powerful fleet had gotten there first. The smaller British force was beaten off by the French in the Battle of the Capes (September 5, 1781) and sailed back to New York. Chesapeake Bay belonged to the visiting French warships.

Washington took time on his way south for a very short visit to his beloved plantation, Mount Vernon, which he hadn't seen since 1775. But he

Mount Vernon Ladies' Association

Mount Vernon, near Alexandria, Virginia. This colonial mansion was George Washington's home from 1754 to 1799, and he is buried here.

had to hurry on, for the French and American armies were forming at Williamsburg, Virginia.

At daybreak on September 28, 1781, a fine, sunny day, the French and Americans marched down the road from Williamsburg to Yorktown. There were more than 8,000 Americans now, combined with France's 7,800 regular army men. At Yorktown, some fourteen miles away, Cornwallis had only 7,000 soldiers. The British were well dug in. Their fortifications were not all finished, but even so, the French and American Allies did not expect to charge the British position. Washington planned a siege.

The first obstacles in Washington's way were three British camps, at a distance of 1,000 yards from Cornwallis' main entrenchments and southwest of Yorktown proper. During the night of September 30th Cornwallis pulled his men back from these exposed outposts.

Washington's men promptly took the camps and started shelling Yorktown from them. Cornwallis' move seemed strange. But he had just received a letter from Clinton, saying that 5,000 British soldiers were on their way to help him. Cornwallis was confident that he could hold out until their arrival, and believed he could withstand the siege better by drawing in all his soldiers in a close, compact formation.

The Allies, after they had taken over the British fortifications, started to build entrenchments of

Brown Brothers

Above: The Yorktown Battlefield, Yorktown, Virginia. Cornwallis' surrender here on October 19, 1781, was, in effect, the end of the war. Here one of the British gun positions is guarded by *chevaux-de-frise*, pointed logs driven into the ground.

Below: The Yorktown Battlefield, Yorktown, Virginia. American and French artillery played an important part in the siege of Yorktown. These guns are placed to fire through openings in the earthen embankment.

Lawrence D. Thornton

their own. The Americans worked on one side of Yorktown, while the French attacked on the other, keeping the British busy and preventing them from concentrating their fire against the American work parties. After the end of the first week in October, the French and American artillerymen, firing around the clock, were able to pour cannon shells into Yorktown at a fierce rate.

Then the Allies began building a second row of trenches, closer to Yorktown than the first.

Cornwallis tried to escape. The reinforcements on which he counted had not appeared. He ordered boats to take his army across the York River on the night of October 16th. A storm blew up; the crossing was impossible, and the next day the British were still in Yorktown.

The Allies were shattering Yorktown with artillery fire. The shelling was so heavy that most of the time Cornwallis' gunners were unable to fire back. Worse still, the British were coming to the end of their ammunition supplies.

Cornwallis gave up. On the morning of the 17th a British drummer climbed onto the fortifications of Yorktown and beat the signal for a parley. The cannons were making so much noise that no one heard him, but the Americans saw him and ceased firing. A British officer came out carrying a white handkerchief. Allied officers led him, blindfolded, to Washington's headquarters.

He told Washington that Cornwallis was ready to surrender.

Officers from both sides met in a handsome white house just outside the town and worked out surrender terms. At two o'clock on the afternoon of October 19, 1781, the British, in brilliant, clean uniforms, marched out of Yorktown between the armies of the Americans and the French, who were drawn up to watch. The British army bands played an old tune called "The World Turned Upside Down." The words of the song mention such upside-down events as mice chasing cats and grass eating cows, and perhaps the defeated British felt that their world had indeed turned upside down.

The Americans and French were well behaved, trying not to insult the soldiers they had defeated. But they looked proud, and they could not conceal their smiles of joy.

Cornwallis did not come out to hand his sword to Washington. He said he was sick, and he asked his second in command, General Charles O'Hara, to make the surrender for him. The British soldiers were marched off to prison camps, but their commanders, including Cornwallis himself, were allowed to return to England once they gave their word not to fight against the Americans again.

On that very day—the day of the surrender— Clinton sailed from New York City with the 7,000 men who were to rescue the garrison at Yorktown. There were 2,000 more men than promised, but they were a little late. Clinton's ships arrived off the Chesapeake Capes five days later. There was nothing, of course, that he could do. He turned around and sailed back to New York.

20
The End of the War

No one realized that Yorktown was the end. Clinton returned to New York. Washington marched north with his army. The French fleet headed back to the West Indies.

Lord North, in London, was one of the few exceptions. When news of Cornwallis' surrender reached him, he cried, "Oh God! It is all over!"

King George was prepared to continue the fight, but he was almost the only man in England who was. Parliament, which voted the money to pay for the war, had had enough. Parliament could stop the war, and it did so. Early in 1782 Parliament declared that anybody who wanted to go on fighting the Americans was an enemy to his country, and it told King George to make peace.

The bitter struggle had lasted far, far longer than expected. British taxes were higher than ever. The war, which was supposed to have lowered them, had raised them instead. And the British feared that America's new friendship with the

145

French might ruin England's profitable American trade.

Peace negotiations started in Paris. They took a long time, and the treaty was not signed until September 3, 1783. It recognized the United States of America as an independent nation that stretched from the Atlantic to the Mississippi. In November the British army left New York City. The Continental Army was disbanded. Washington, its great leader, went home to Mount Vernon. He looked forward to a well-earned rest as a private citizen and a chance to get his plantation back in shape. He had no idea that his country would call him into service again as its first President.

American independence, the fruit of the struggle that had started in 1760, set a new task—the job of writing a Constitution and giving form to the ideas of self-government that had gradually developed.

Even while the American Revolution was being fought, America's leaders knew that their ideas of liberty had come from England, their temporary enemy. The entire shape of the new government of the United States—from the county, which was a British unit, to the various parts of the federal government itself—was to show the influence of British forms.

The fact was that, despite the war, the people in England on one hand, and the Americans and French on the other, were moving in similar directions. King George's attempt to win more power for the Crown failed, and the British were working out their government in which "the King reigns, but does not rule." France, too, was on the point of developing her system of political democracy. The three nations that fought the Revolutionary War, linked by their common ideals and governed by men their own citizens had elected, were to become firm friends and constant allies.

The American Revolution was fought for more than mere independence from Great Britain, and it achieved something beyond one new country on the map of the world.

A particular kind of new country was established—a nation in which every human being could be free, and have something to say about how he or she was governed.

ℰ Index

References to illustrations are in *italic type.*

149

❧ About the Author

Bruce Bliven, Jr., has had a long and productive writing career. He began as a reporter for the English newspaper the Manchester *Guardian* and then became a writer for the New York *Post*. Drawing on his own experience as a soldier in World War II, he wrote three Landmark Books about that war: *From Casablanca to Berlin, The Story of D-Day,* and *From Pearl Harbor to Okinawa*. Since the war, he has written a number of other books as well as scores of articles and reviews for many national magazines including *Atlantic, Harper's, Esquire, Saturday Review,* and *The New York Times Book Review*.

Mr. Bliven is a staff contributor to *The New Yorker* magazine. He lives with his wife and co-author, Naomi, and his college-age son in New York City.